Songs from the Front Lawn

T0274864

33 1/3 Global

33 1/3 Global, a series related to but independent from **33 1/3**, takes the format of the original series of short, music-based books and brings the focus to music throughout the world. With initial volumes focusing on Japanese and Brazilian music, the series will also include volumes on the popular music of Australia/Oceania, Europe, Africa, the Middle East, and more.

33 1/3 Japan

Series Editor: Noriko Manabe

Spanning a range of artists and genres – from the 1970s rock of Happy End to technopop band Yellow Magic Orchestra, the Shibuya-kei of Cornelius, classic anime series *Cowboy Bebop,* J-Pop/EDM hybrid Perfume, and vocaloid star Hatsune Miku – 33 1/3 Japan is a series devoted to in-depth examination of Japanese popular music of the twentieth and twenty-first centuries.

Published Titles:

Supercell's *Supercell* by Keisuke Yamada

AKB48 by Patrick W. Galbraith and Jason G. Karlin

Yoko Kanno's *Cowboy Bebop Soundtrack* by Rose Bridges

Perfume's *Game* by Patrick St. Michel

Cornelius's *Fantasma* by Martin Roberts

Joe Hisaishi's *My Neighbor Totoro: Soundtrack* by Kunio Hara

Shonen Knife's *Happy Hour* by Brooke McCorkle

Nenes' *Koza Dabasa* by Henry Johnson

Yuming's *The 14th Moon* by Lasse Lehtonen

Forthcoming Titles:

Yellow Magic Orchestra's *Yellow Magic Orchestra* by Toshiyuki Ohwada

Kohaku utagassen: The Red and White Song Contest by Shelley Brunt

33 1/3 Brazil

Series Editor: Jason Stanyek

Covering the genres of samba, tropicália, rock, hip hop, forró, bossa nova, heavy metal and funk, among others, 33 1/3 Brazil is a series devoted to in-depth examination of the most important Brazilian albums of the twentieth and twenty-first centuries.

Published Titles:

Caetano Veloso's *A Foreign Sound* by Barbara Browning

Tim Maia's *Tim Maia Racional Vols. 1 &2* by Allen Thayer

João Gilberto and Stan Getz's *Getz/Gilberto* by Brian McCann

Gilberto Gil's *Refazenda* by Marc A. Hertzman

Dona Ivone Lara's *Sorriso Negro* by Mila Burns

Milton Nascimento and Lô Borges's *The Corner Club* by Jonathon Grasse

Racionais MCs' *Sobrevivendo no Inferno* by Derek Pardue

Naná Vasconcelos's *Saudades* by Daniel B. Sharp

Chico Buarque's First *Chico Buarque* by Charles A. Perrone

Forthcoming titles:

Jorge Ben Jor's *África Brasil* by Frederick J. Moehn

33 1/3 Europe

Series Editor: Fabian Holt

Spanning a range of artists and genres, 33 1/3 Europe offers engaging accounts of popular and culturally significant albums of Continental Europe and the North Atlantic from the twentieth and twenty-first centuries.

Published Titles:

Darkthrone's *A Blaze in the Northern Sky* by Ross Hagen

Ivo Papazov's *Balkanology* by Carol Silverman

Heiner Müller and Heiner Goebbels's *Wolokolamsker Chaussee* by Philip V. Bohlman

Modeselektor's *Happy Birthday!* by Sean Nye

Mercyful Fate's *Don't Break the Oath* by Henrik Marstal

Bea Playa's *I'll Be Your Plaything* by Anna Szemere and András Rónai

Various Artists' *DJs do Guetto* by Richard Elliott

Czesław Niemen's *Niemen Enigmatic* by Ewa Mazierska and Mariusz Gradowski

Massada's *Astaganaga* by Lutgard Mutsaers

Los Rodriguez's *Sin Documentos* by Fernán del Val and Héctor Fouce

Édith Piaf's *Récital 1961* by David Looseley
Nuovo Canzoniere Italiano's *Bella Ciao* by Jacopo Tomatis
Iannis Xenakis' *Persepolis* by Aram Yardumian

Forthcoming Titles:
Amália Rodrigues's *Amália at the Olympia* by Lila Ellen Gray
Ardit Gjebrea's *Projekt Jon* by Nicholas Tochka
Vopli Vidopliassova's *Tantsi* by Maria Sonevytsky

33 1/3 Oceania

Series Editors: Jon Stratton (senior editor) and Jon Dale (specializing in books on albums from Aotearoa/New Zealand)

Spanning a range of artists and genres from Australian Indigenous artists to Maori and Pasifika artists, from Aotearoa/New Zealand noise music to Australian rock, and including music from Papua and other Pacific islands, 33 1/3 Oceania offers exciting accounts of albums that illustrate the wide range of music made in the Oceania region.

Published Titles:
John Farnham's *Whispering Jack* by Graeme Turner
The Church's *Starfish* by Chris Gibson
Regurgitator's *Unit* by Lachlan Goold and Lauren Istvandity
Kylie Minogue's *Kylie* by Adrian Renzo and Liz Giuffre
Alastair Riddell's *Space Waltz* by Ian Chapman
Hunters & Collectors's *Human Frailty* by Jon Stratton
The Front Lawn's *Songs from the Front Lawn* by Matthew Bannister

Forthcoming Titles:
Ed Kuepper's *Honey Steel's Gold* by John Encarnacao
The Dead C's *Clyma est mort* by Darren Jorgensen
Chain's *Toward the Blues* by Peter Beilharz
Bic Runga's *Drive* by Henry Johnson
Hilltop Hoods' *The Calling* by Dianne Rodger
Screamfeeder's *Kitten Licks* by Ben Green and Ian Rogers
Luke Rowell's *Buy Now* by Michael Brown

Songs from the Front Lawn

Matthew Bannister

Series Editors: Jon Stratton, UniSA Creative, University of South Australia, and Jon Dale, University of Melbourne, Australia

BLOOMSBURY ACADEMIC
NEW YORK • LONDON • OXFORD • NEW DELHI • SYDNEY

BLOOMSBURY ACADEMIC
Bloomsbury Publishing Inc
1385 Broadway, New York, NY 10018, USA
50 Bedford Square, London, WC1B 3DP, UK
29 Earlsfort Terrace, Dublin 2, Ireland

BLOOMSBURY, BLOOMSBURY ACADEMIC and the Diana logo are trademarks
of Bloomsbury Publishing Plc

First published in the United States of America 2023
Reprinted 2023

For legal purposes the Acknowledgements on p. ix constitute an extension of
this copyright page.

Cover design: John Reynolds
Cover image © John Reynolds

Library of Congress Cataloging-in-Publication Data
Names: Bannister, Matthew, author.
Title: Songs from the Front Lawn / Matthew Bannister.
Description: New York, NY : Bloomsbury Academic, 2023. |
Series: 33 1/3 Oceania | Includes bibliographical references and index. |
Summary: "An in-depth discussion of an album that encapsulates being a
Pakeha New Zealander in the 1980s"– Provided by publisher.
Identifiers: LCCN 2022043232 (print) | LCCN 2022043233 (ebook) |
ISBN 9781501390081 (hardback) | ISBN 9781501390098 (paperback) |
ISBN 9781501390104 (epub) | ISBN 9781501390111
(pdf) | ISBN 9781501390128 (ebook other)
Subjects: LCSH: Front Lawn (Musical group). Songs From the Front Lawn. |
Popular music–New Zealand–1981-1990–History and criticism.
Classification: LCC ML421.F76 B35 2023 (print) | LCC ML421.F76 (ebook) |
DDC 782.421640993–dc23/eng/20220916
LC record available at https://lccn.loc.gov/2022043232
LC ebook record available at https://lccn.loc.gov/2022043233

ISBN: HB: 978-1-5013-9008-1
          PB: 978-1-5013-9009-8
          ePDF: 978-1-5013-9011-1
          eBook: 978-1-5013-9010-4

Series: 33 1/3 Oceania

Typeset by Integra Software Services Pvt. Ltd.
Printed and bound in the Great Britain

To find out more about our authors and books visit www.bloomsbury.com and
sign up for our newsletters.

Contents

List of figures

Images: All photos are by John Reynolds unless otherwise credited; all photos are property of The Front Lawn.

Acknowledgements

The Author wishes to acknowledge the help of The Front Lawn (Don McGlashan, Harry Sinclair and Jennifer Ward-Lealand) and David Long in writing this book. Also Wintec/Te Pūkenga which gave me research time to write it.

Note on typography symbols. I have used macrons, e.g. 'ā', in Māori words, except for quotes where macrons were not used.

1   Background

'The only thing I get from the theatre', said Paul McCartney to playwright Joe Orton in the heyday of Swinging London, 'is a sore arse'.[1] My sentiments, in somewhat less swinging Dunedin/ Ōtepoti, were similar, but Don McGlashan's involvement in *The Reason for Breakfast*, at the Allen Theatre at the University of Otago in November 1986, changed things. He had contributed euphonium and percussion to my band's last album (Sneaky Feelings' *Sentimental Education*) – one instrument he had used was an iron skillet, a clue as to what I was about to witness. McGlashan had also written and sung 'Don't Fight It Marsha, It's Bigger Than Both of Us' a 1981 track by his band Blam Blam Blam. Accessible and arty, familiar and strange, punk and progressive, and with a suitably enigmatic video (also McGlashan's first collaboration with Harry Sinclair) it was a blueprint for NZ music in the 1980s.

This was pre-internet times; hence I went to my first Front Lawn show totally clueless. The lights went up on two men at a breakfast table, but rather than talking to each other, they did things. McGlashan started tapping on a milk bottle, Sinclair started humming and soon they were both singing and hitting things – transforming the breakfast table into a symphony of the everyday. 'We are the milky tea drinkers … Isn't this great?' they sang, 'see all the things we've got, this bottle, this plate, see the way the light shines through this jam jar!' It was absurd, funny and curiously life-affirming. The only other local plays I had seen were Bruce Mason's *Blood of the Lamb* (1981) and Greg McGee's *Foreskin's Lament* (1981), and they were pretty grim. What a relief to see a show that made you feel good. But it wasn't just a laugh: there was energy and excitement, and, of course, reason (for breakfast). Murray Edmond writes that 'inside the work of the … Front Lawn we will find an image of paradise', because The Front Lawn derive from Commedia Dell 'Arte, semi-improvised comedy that mixes the 'skilled actor' – literally someone who performs a skill onstage (like a musician), and the 'personal actor', who is 'tied on stage to the name, the identity which marked his offstage life'.[2] McGlashan and Sinclair referred to each other onstage as Don and Harry, Edmond commenting how the duo 'work by opposition. Harry is tall, Don is short; Harry is suave, ingratiating, a little too slick to be trustworthy, but an excellent communicator; [whereas] Don is naïve, honest, lacking in finesse'.[3]

I had never seen anything quite like it, and that was only the first half. The second part was a series of skits and songs,

Figure 1.1 *The Front Lawn – Don McGlashan (left) and Harry Sinclair (right) perform c. 1985.*

alternately hilarious and moving. 'I'm Right' was a song/skit built around the repeated title phrase. The duo strode around the stage, pointing at things, shouting, 'Look at that!', 'What did I tell you?' folding their arms, nodding, winking, grimacing, finally pronouncing, 'Everything about me tells me I'm right!' It was a brilliant parody of Kiwi bloke masculinity (later made into a music video). It reminds me now of the party scene in Taika Waititi's *Eagle vs. Shark* (2007) when Jarod (Jemaine Clement) is talking to Lily (Loren Horsley) about her costume: 'It's pretty much the second-best outfit here. I almost came as a shark, actually … but then I realized that an eagle is *slightly better.*' In his slacker way, Jarod is just as arrogant as McGlashan and Sinclair's righteous blokes. But there were also moments of bizarre beauty – a song about the French police inspector in *Casablanca*, or more accurately, the actor playing him, Claude Rains. Intertextual references (as we now know them) were rare in NZ art at that time. Everyone seemed obsessed with proving how local they were, and referring to something foreign without condemning it was almost unheard of. It was such a relief to see a performance that seemed relaxed about saying, yes, we watch films; yes, we are aware of the world outside New Zealand. At the same time, McGlashan and Harry in their check shirts, were 'Kiwi as'. But they were also new.

New Zealand/Aotearoa in the 1980s was a country in reluctant but increasingly rapid transformation, dating from 1973 when the United Kingdom, New Zealand's no. 1 export market, joined the EEC. NZ historian James Belich termed the entire period from the turn of the century to the 1970s 'recolonization',[4] when New Zealand continued to enjoy a cosy but rather incestuous relationship with its original colonizer: 'Geographically it may have been in the Pacific, but structurally it was part of Britain's rural hinterland.'[5] NZ lamb, beef, butter and cheese filled British larders, making New Zealand one of the most prosperous post-war countries. In turn, New Zealand imported British culture – TV, films, books and received pronunciation continued to dominate local life, whatever part of it was not filled by the United States. New Zealanders remained British subjects until 1983. Cultural cringe ran rampant. The apron strings had never really been cut. To paraphrase Philip Larkin, New Zealand began in 1973. But it was still-born – in 1975, Robert Muldoon was elected NZ Prime Minister. Muldoon promised his followers, known as Rob's Mob, a security blanket against the loss of overseas markets and the turbulent post Bretton Woods global economic environment, by creating Fortress New Zealand, an economy heavily protected by import duties. Muldoon was a state interventionist with a conservative agenda, a right-wing leader who also wanted to control the economy. Moreover, he was divisive – liberals and minorities hated his autocratic style, and he bullied at least one potential opposition leader out of Parliament in 1977 when he accused Labour shadow cabinet MP Colin Moyle of being homosexual (homosexuality was not legalized in New Zealand until 1986).

Muldoon, a Pākehā (white settler), also crossed swords with New Zealand's indigenous inhabitants, Māori, who since the 1950s had been steadily migrating into the cities in search of work, along with similarly motivated immigration from the Pacific Islands, which exacerbated racial tension. In 1975, a Māori woman leader, Dame Whina Cooper, led a Land March the length of the North Island/Te Ika-a-Māui to Wellington/Te Whanganui-a-Tara, the NZ capital, to present a petition demanding return of Māori land. The Treaty of Waitangi Act 1975 established a legal process for investigating historic claims by Māori against the Crown. The 1970s saw a

Māori Renaissance (Taha Māori): a rediscovery of Māori art, language and culture.[6] Māori urban protest movements such as Ngā Tamatoa (Young Warriors) emerged, counting future Māori filmmakers like Merata Mita and Barry Barclay among their members, and this led to significant interactions with ideas of blackness (from the United States), with Pasifika activists (the Polynesian Panthers) and with Rastafarianism and reggae music.

Muldoon continued the policy of Dawn Raids in which Pasifika households were invaded by police and 'overstayers' summarily deported. At Bastion Point, Auckland/Tāmaki Makaurau, in 1978, he ended a 505-day Māori land protest with police arrests. Implicitly his 'Government of the ordinary bloke'[2] was a government of the white bloke. Ethnic tensions came to a head in 1981, with the Springbok Tour. Muldoon allowed representatives of apartheid, the South African rugby team to play in New Zealand, which made him popular with his constituents but infuriated many among ethnic minorities, liberals, left-wingers and young people, and a series of violent confrontations ensued, mostly between anti-tour protesters and police. Muldoon continued to rule until 1984, when he called a snap election after a confrontation with a government backbencher Marilyn Waring on another 1980s-defining issue, the nuclear-free New Zealand bill, which rejected military ties with the United States and protested French nuclear testing in the Pacific. Muldoon lost the election to the Labour Party, who promptly implemented neoliberal free-market policies, selling State assets, and deregulating financial markets, an approach that became known as 'Rogernomics', after its architect, finance minister Roger Douglas (with obvious resemblances to Reaganomics). So, a conservative, right-wing, interventionist government was replaced by a liberal, left-wing, free-market government. Only in NZ …

The second paradox of NZ politics, as noted by McGlashan, in a 1988 interview with Australian theatre publication *ANT News*, is the 'difference between New Zealand's foreign policy, which presents an orientation to the left, and its domestic policy, which has seen a big swing to the right. Consequently, this is a very difficult time for the arts. The per capita funding … is much lower than in Australia.'[7] Culturally, the idea of national identity was becoming more prominent, even though NZ leaders like Muldoon continued to refer to Britain as the 'mother country'.[8] But what kind of an identity was it to be? The most original aspect of NZ identity was clearly its indigenous people, but after over a century of unlicensed exploitation, Māori were increasingly chary of Pākehā appropriation of their assets and culture. Even well-meaning types like journalist Michael King, a driving force behind the groundbreaking 1974 TV documentary series *Tangata Whenua*, noted that 'in 1971 the Maori radicals were arguing that Pakeha historians had neglected Maori history … [but] … as a consequence of the rise of mana Maori the argument was no longer that Pakeha historians should write about Maori history; it was that they should not'.[9] This hands-off attitude was understandable; at the same time, it encouraged Pākehā to think about their cultural identity separate from Māori, which was not necessarily a good thing.

Pākehā cultural nationalism emerged mainly in the arts and found powerful support in the form of poet and academic Keith Sinclair, also a 'founding father' of NZ history.[10] Sinclair's histories of New Zealand were informed by a narrative of NZ independence; his last book was called *A Destiny Apart: New Zealand's Search for National Identity*.[11] The identity that emerged was characteristically that of the 'ordinary' or Kiwi bloke, a 'man alone', usually white, rural, pragmatic and laconic.[12] Sinclair married Mary Edith Land in 1947 and they had four sons, the youngest of whom was christened Harry, born in Auckland in 1959. An interest in the arts informed the whole family – older brother Stephen co-wrote New Zealand's most commercially successful play, *Ladies Night* (1987). 'Books were very important to my father', comments Harry. 'Like something sacred. For him they were the answer to every problem. If my father was annoyed with us because we were too noisy, he would yell, "Get yourself a book!" For a bookish man he was very loud … we lived in Takapuna. I think my parents chose that suburb because it was regarded as the place writers lived.'[13]

Don McGlashan was also born in Auckland in 1959; his mother was a schoolteacher and his father taught civil engineering at Auckland Technical Institute. 'My Dad wanted me to learn a musical instrument, so he kept bringing old, secondhand musical instruments to the house … So by the time I got to intermediate school, I was dragged into various bands because I could play a few things.'[14] He attended Westlake Boys High School on Auckland's North Shore, where he combined playing in orchestras with playing in garage bands. Also at Westlake was Sinclair, though the two students were a year apart, and as McGlashan explains, 'You could lose a lot of points socially for fraternizing with someone younger than you.' Nevertheless, their paths crossed:

> McGlashan: Harry … wrote a rock opera … with a friend of mine called Scott Calhoun. It was called *Chewing a Tulip* and it had a great final scene where one of the … protagonists totally loses it and shouts 'Shit! Shit! Shit!' and the heavens open and a whole bunch of shit falls on him …. It was performed twice.

Sinclair: I went to a farm and got lots of cow dung and put it
up above the stage … I had to do the show twice because
my parents were divorced and I wanted them both to see it.

McGlashan: They couldn't be in the same room together.

Sinclair: I played my father, satirising him in quite a vicious way.[15]

Punk

The ultimate expression of parricide, punk rock arrived in
mainstream New Zealand in March 1977 via local TV current
affairs programme *Eye Witness* – the Sex Pistols performed
'Anarchy in the UK' in an item detailing this latest British craze.[16]
It coincided with a new emphasis on everyday experience and
quotidian reality in French writers like Michel de Certeau
and Henri Lefebvre, incorporating local features like accents
and placenames as resistance to global capitalism: 'Only in
the local network of labor and recreation can one grasp how,
within a grid of socio-economic constraints, these pursuits
unfailingly establish relational tactics (a struggle for life),
artistic creations (an aesthetic), and autonomous initiatives (an
ethic).'[17] Free local music paper *Rip It Up* first appeared in June
1977, to document a burgeoning local scene. McGlashan first
played in a school rock band called Ethos; Sinclair comments:
'I claim to have invented that name', and McGlashan responds,
'What a terrible thing to claim.'[18] Soon McGlashan became
involved with another ex-Westlake Boys student, Richard Von
Sturmer and his band The Plague (with whom Von Sturmer
appeared naked and painted blue at the Nambassa Festival
in 1979), alternating between punk gigs and playing French
horn in the Auckland Symphonia. The Auckland punk scene

spawned a number of groups including the Scavengers and the Suburban Reptiles, who released New Zealand's first punk single 'Saturday Night Stay at Home' (Phonogram 1978). John Dix, who wrote the first history of NZ rock, *Stranded in Paradise*, opined that 'New Zealand kids embraced punk … only Presley and the Beatles have had a greater impact on the local scene than the Sex Pistols.'[19]

Wellington had its own punk HQ, 212 The Terrace, a flat which included such future luminaries as screenwriter Fran Walsh (*The Lord of the Rings*) and future Front Lawn member Jennifer Ward-Lealand. Punk valued amateurism over professionalism – anyone could have a go, including women. Both Walsh and Ward-Lealand performed in punk band Naked Spots Dance, and the flat also included members of the Wallsockets, Life in the Fridge Exists, Shoes This High and Riot 111. Ward-Lealand: 'It was a very band oriented house … so when McGlashan was in Blam Blam Blam, they'd been through at some stage; I'm talking 1980–81.'

Blam Blam Blam were more post-punk than punk, the trio emerging from the ashes of the Plague, with McGlashan on drums and vocals, Mark Bell on guitar and Tim Mahon on bass. McGlashan had never actually played a drum kit before: 'I locked myself away in Frank Stark and Mary-Louise Brown's warehouse gallery on Federal Street for a few weeks, and learnt how to play kit by listening to The Specials, Booker T and The MGs and Clash records.'[20] The group became a cultural touchstone in the turbulence of 1981 via 'There is No Depression in New Zealand', a heavily sardonic update of comedian Fred Dagg (John Clarke)'s 1975 NZ comedy anthem, 'We Don't Know How Lucky We Are'. This McGlashan/Von Sturmer music/lyrics collaboration, released on Simon Grigg's Auckland indie Propeller Records, reached no. 11 in the singles charts. The Blams infused the basic rock trio format with reggae rhythms and social comment, e.g. 'Got To Be Guilty', 'Respect', both of which commented on authoritarianism in New Zealand (Blam Blam Blam mini LP, Propeller, 1982). Reggae was the music of protest in 1981 New Zealand, and can be heard in Merata Mita's Springbok Tour documentary, *Patu!* It was also popular with Māori/Pasifika, leading to bands like Herbs, Twelve Tribes of Israel, Aotearoa and Dread, Beat & Blood.[21] At the same time, its influence also seeped into post-punk via the UK two-tone sound of bands like the Specials. However, with the ascension of South Island indie labels like Flying Nun from 1982, post-punk (or as it became known, alternative) music got whiter. South Island/Te Waipounamu demography was one reason, but also, in line with Michael King's comment, there was an element of 'not pretending to be black' in the post-punk scene, including rejection of 1970s pub rock, which had a strong blues (and therefore ultimately black) influence. Although commentary on everyday life was to become part of The Front Lawn, it sometimes lacked the political and satirical overtones of this early work, product of a particularly polarizing time. At the same time, relationship (or lack of) to the country's indigenous culture was to become an issue as New Zealand moved towards biculturalism from the 1980s onward.

But just as important as ethnicity was gender: 'We have no racism, we have no sexism', as 'There is No Depression' sarcastically states. Sexism and racism were the two biggest issues on university campuses in the early 1980s. Many young people were in revolt against traditional gender roles, and in New Zealand there was a particularly strong reaction against Muldoon and his 'ordinary bloke' followers, who were identified with a xenophobic, homophobic masculinity. This in turn correlated to cultural stereotypes such as the Kiwi bloke, the tough, laconic, usually rural, DIY type; the rugby, racing and beer generation, a stereotype reinforced by the Springbok tour protests.

> Sinclair: We … played a lot with the question of what masculinity means in NZ, having both of us struggled to fit in. It's extremely hard to be a man in NZ, because it's a very narrow field, or at least it used to be … Any divergence would be seen as gay, weird … unacceptable, I grew up feeling extremely constrained by the NZ ideal of masculinity.

In contrast, The Front Lawn 'celebrated what it was like to be a bloke in NZ in an intelligent and nice manner'.[22] A number of Front Lawn works were to address this issue, and not unrelatedly, the group added Jennifer Ward-Lealand in 1988, as they recorded their first album.

Sinclair spent the early 1980s acting in an Auckland company called Theatre Corporate:

> [A] small, almost microscopic theatre which led to an intense, psychological approach … very Stanislavski … very scientific, and ultimately … very tiresome. What I found most exciting in theatre were those things that happened by mistake … I saw a show called *Jumping Mouse* by Jon Bolton … he had studied at Le Coq in Paris so I … ended up studying with Phillipe Gaulier and Monika Pagneux … a totally different approach to theatre which was much more external … just coming on stage and being entertaining.[23]

Apparently on their first meeting, Gaulier informed Sinclair that he had 'swallowed an umbrella', a French expression meaning 'uptight'. 'Harry', he said, 'you carry the burden of the Commonwealth'.[24] McGlashan was also very busy in the early 1980s, as besides all the activities listed above, he was also a member of a key experimental music ensemble, From Scratch.

Founded by sonic artist Phil Dadson in 1974, the group were best known for producing polyrhythmic, percussion-based works, often using variable lengths of plastic tubing, played with jandals. This gave the work a distinctively NZ DIY flavour (which they stressed by making assembly of the instruments part of the performance) but they were also influenced by a Solomon Islands group performing with bamboo tube instruments at the 1976 South Pacific Festival of the Arts in Rotorua.[25] So, once again, cultural appropriation was an issue. Earlier works had revealed influences from the avant-garde classical world such as Cornelius Cardew, Philip Glass and John Cage, but emphasis on rhythm was to become the From Scratch trademark. It continued to be important in The Front Lawn, who often used repeating/intertwining patterns at a micro and macro level, whether musical or temporal; the rhythms of music or of everyday life, such as rituals. Such practice is in line with the contemporaneous development of rhythmanalysis:

> An approach to everyday life that focuses on the effects of rhythms on people and the places they occupy. It was developed by Henri Lefebvre in *Rhythmanalysis: Space, Time and Everyday Life* ... and focuses on the cyclical and linear rhythms that structure the body and everyday behaviour. Cyclical rhythms are repetitious, such as night into day and day into night, or the times of meals. Linear rhythms might be the flow of traffic along a road.[26]

From Scratch opened up McGlashan to new influences:

> I was really interested in a kind of compositional, mathematical, philosophical, political way, and From Scratch was a juncture of all these ideas, and opened me up to the visual arts world because we'd go to these festivals and we'd be in panels with

all these painters and looking at their practice and what they were trying to do. I've not got much of a visual sense but could appreciate all the things that you have in common when you're painting, trying to grab the world and filter it through your craft and put it on a canvas.[27]

Elsewhere he has commented: 'We treat our shows like rhythm pieces. Language is rhythm; human beings are rhythmic objects. In performing … we are … taking a chunk of time out of the audience's day and dividing it up into a series of musical shapes.'[28]

Sinclair and McGlashan first collaborated in 1981, on the video clip of Blam Blam Blam's 'Don't Fight It Marsha, It's Bigger Than Both of Us', with its neurotic, distracted lyric, which McGlashan described as 'an imitation of early Talking Heads … where you have a really unsympathetic character standing up and stating his case', and a lengthy coda, dominated by an epic, looping euphonium melody (also played by McGlashan).[29] It established him as a major NZ songwriter, winning Song of the Year in the 1982 New Zealand Recording Industry Awards. Of the clip, he says: 'I wanted some faces on screen, so I asked Harry … and [he] came up with a bunch of actors pulling the same faces or responding to the same story … [he] directed them off-camera.' Sinclair says, 'It was supposed to be like a grid of faces but we didn't have the video technology to create a grid … [NZ actors] Donna Reese, Michael Hurst and Phil Gordon [appeared].'[30] The Blams released an album, *Luxury Length*, on Propeller Records, in May 1982, though the cost of the recording precipitated a financial crisis for their label, given the small NZ market. The band ground to a halt after a 1982 car accident in which bassist Tim Mahon lost a finger, although they have reformed on several occasions.[31]

McGlashan: Then we both went overseas [McGlashan initially with From Scratch], and … met up briefly in New York, and … again in London, while we were both on our OE … (Harry) must have been in London longer than me; I was in New York through 1982 and 1983, and then I went back to London with From Scratch for the Edinburgh Festival and that's when we met up, in a cheese shop.

Sinclair: I was in Paris for a year studying drama, 1983–4, then I worked in a cheese shop in London; I recommended cheeses to him which he proceeded to buy, which was really a turning point … The passing of the cheese in return for English sterling.[32] I saw [Don] there and I saw [him] in New York – I remember cycling, rather terrified, around the streets of New York with [Don] in September 1983.

McGlashan: I was in the Laura Dean Dancers and Musicians, I was holding down this gig as a percussionist in a dance company … repetitive, very rhythmic work. We toured Europe in 1983 and did two American tours.[33] The following year (1984) we met in London … I think we both knew we were going to go back to New Zealand … I wanted to make music but I didn't really wanna be in a band … Harry had been in a theatre company and he felt the same way about that … New Zealanders are like … sponges … overseas … When I first got [to NY] I wanted to write great soul songs … and I wanted to know everything about Jewish stand-up comedy – but [eventually] I thought I should use what's unique about me … Harry and I were united by … wanting to talk about where we grew up – to find a style that came from us.[34]

2   The Front Lawn

Whence the front lawn? According to Virginia Jenkins, 'In the 18th century … wealthy Americans emulated the landscape of English country estates.'[1] The lawn represented genteel aspirations. By the twentieth century, 'magazine readers were told that a good lawn represented good citizenship in transient communities in which residents were judged on the appearance of the home from the street'.[2] The lawn is both private and public property: 'the notion of ownership … confused by two competing rights: the rights of those who inhabit the property versus the rights of those who view the property'.[3]

> Sinclair: [The name] was a metaphor for the clipped nature of New Zealand culture, keeping nature under control. [It was also about] looking at the small details of life, examining wider themes by looking at the minutiae of the world … it was a suburban thing, we did shows about breakfast, about smallish, domestic things. [It also reflected NZ's green-ness.] Returning from overseas, you look out the plane window and NZ just looks like a big lawn … Most New Zealand babies hear lawnmowers before they hear radios. It's not until much later that they learn one is music and one isn't … we've long felt that what we're brought up to believe is an ugly sound is actually a meaningful cultural expression. The chorus of lawnmowers on Saturday morning is the closest thing we have to communal music.[4]

Figure 2.1 *Those green lawn jackets – at the Auckland University Student's Union, 1985.*

McGlashan [to Sinclair]: The piece with the sheep and the green furry jackets, did you come up with that?

Sinclair: [NZ actor] Alison Wall made us these big, bright green, fur jackets and we came on to the stage with our hands in our pockets and then … we'd bring our hands out and we'd have white gloves on and our hands would roam around our bodies and we made sheep noises.

McGlashan: As we say in the theatre, it was execution dependent.

It would have been possible for the duo to stay abroad, but something drew them back to New Zealand.

> McGlashan: It was a moment when we first saw New Zealand with very new eyes, and … with a lot of ideas about what performance could be … When I was in New York I looked a lot at Laurie Anderson … looking at a power point [electrical socket] and then blowing it up so it's the size of the stage – just changing the scale of an object can really change how you feel about it. But at the same time, I got really involved in Irish folk music … people telling stories of longing and distance through very simple songs … a Front Lawn show could encompass all those things.

> Sinclair: It was like a moment of 'anything is possible', and we'd seen a lot of interesting things, performance art and music, came back to NZ very inspired, like what can we do with this stuff that we've learned, equipped to speak about New Zealand with a new voice … I didn't really like theatre, and from the beginning of The Front Lawn we tried never to use the word 'theatre'; we used the word 'show'.

However, it was not immediately obvious what the show would be. For example, if music was involved, there was all the paraphernalia of electronic amplification:

> Sinclair: We were performing one of our very first shows at the Fortune Theatre in Dunedin and we had amps and a number of electronic things that all failed the moment we stepped onstage and Don disappeared under a curtain … I was left facing the audience with only Don's feet as he tried to plug things in, and for me that was the crucial moment, because everyone started laughing and the mood was like, what the fuck, it doesn't matter about the gear, we were just going to be entertaining.[5]

McGlashan: The audience taught us … we thought we were going to do some quite intense and difficult kind of performance art-y sort of things, but as soon as we stood up in front of people, they laughed, and [we thought] … we've got 'em laughing, and then we'll tell them these stories. We'd do some stuff which is about unpacking ritual … about memory, but the fact that they were laughing gave us licence to do those things … the humour's not really on the album, but 'How You Doing' has flashes of it.

Their early live experiences also shaped their views about the relation of music to performance:

McGlashan: I began to be very frustrated by bands – I felt restricted by the technology … the forest of microphones in front. I wanted something that would be as musical as a band but more flexible.[6] We had this quite rigid rule that we would only perform acoustically … or a tiny little guitar amp and we'd sing over it … very flexible … on a dime, you could switch from character to song … Or we'd tell a story and accompany it at the same time. Harry would have his concertina and I would have a guitar and we would both be acting roles and as it got dramatic, we would be doing the score … and sometimes it would morph into a song.

Sinclair: I think we were trying to weave them together in every way we could imagine … we both loved the power of how music could bring a story to life.

McGlashan: Many of the songs were not part of a show as such, though we performed them. Often the link was quite tangential, it could be that two characters were walking down the street and they passed a singer, who was singing a song, which could be 'Claude Rains'.

Sinclair: We were trying to do so many things … sometimes they didn't gel entirely, so one of the nice things about the album is that it takes one aspect of our work … sometimes we would have these radical shifts in our stage act, we'd move from a silly skit to a very maudlin song and the audience could not follow these tonal shifts … Something like 'Andy' didn't always fit into the humorous tone we'd created.

Their early NZ tours gave rise to many memorable experiences. On one occasion, they played Stewart Island/ Rakiura, where they crammed 50 patrons into a hotel dining room to watch them perform on a stage they'd made from beer crates. McGlashan says: 'We managed to get the fluorescent lights in the beer fridge turned off so we could get some semblance of a blackout.' After three days in town they knew some of the locals and were able to point out latecomers by name. During *The Reason for Breakfast* people 'recognized things like the yawns or forgetting the butter goes on before the jam and would yell out things like "that's just like you, Bill,"' added Sinclair.[7]

There was a good deal of experimentation in early Front Lawn shows, partly according to the nature of the audience – at a show in the University of Auckland Student Union in 1985, for example, McGlashan included 'This Is A Love Song', a semi-experimental piece he had recorded for a 1982 Propeller EP *Standards* with Ivan Zagni. Furthermore, the duo used a tape recorder to record loops live (anticipating today's looping pedals) for a number called 'Won't Lie Down': 'rhythm tracks, melodies and harmonies were laid on tape layer after layer.'[8] The show also featured a rare example of satire, a song called 'The Petition' in which the duo showed their support for the

Homosexual Law Reform Act (which was passed the following year). I wonder if they did that one on Stewart Island?

Because the group did not video their performances (they felt that it did not do justice to the audience interaction), many Front Lawn sketches and songs are now lost, including the percussive 'Bones' (which saw the duo playing syndrums), which included the lines 'If it weren't for my bones I'd be just like jelly/I'd have to stay at home and watch the telly', and a homage to the duo's roots, 'There's Something in the Wind on the North Shore.'

Although the album was to be the first recording the group produced for sale, they had already made two short films and a music video. First was the music video for 'I'm Right', directed by Grant Campbell, based on the song/routine from their live show.[9] The music was recorded by McGlashan on his Akai

Figure 2.2 *North Shore boys – map superimposed.*

12-track digital recorder, and had an electronic sound quite unlike the album (but not dissimilar to the duo's second album *More Songs From The Front Lawn*).

> McGlashan: Most people when they make a video, they make an album first, then they choose a single, and they make a video clip of that single, whereas we had an idea for a video (first) and we'll make it a single, and we told people and they said, 'Is there an album?' and we said 'No.' We never even made a single, just the video, and by the time we made the album we'd kind of moved on.

Early digital effects were used to multiply the duo, who chase each other's copies round the screen, like Talking Heads 'Once in a Lifetime' video (1984), which shared similar themes of unconventional masculine bodies in motion, repetition and the strangeness of the everyday. Next was their first short film, ironically titled *Walkshort*.[10]

Shot on Auckland's Karangahape Rd. in early 1987, the film introduced themes of repetition, circularity and, of course, walking, recalling Michel De Certeau's essay on the negotiation of urban space, 'Walking in the City':

> The ordinary practitioners of the city live 'down below', below the thresholds at which visibility begins. They walk – an elementary form of this experience of the city; they are walkers, *Wandersmanner*, whose bodies follow the thicks and thins of an urban 'text' they write without being able to read it. These practitioners make use of spaces that cannot be seen; their knowledge of them is as blind as that of lovers in each other's arms.[11]

Sinclair came up with the circular narrative: 'We were always intrigued by time but I don't know what the hell we were saying about it.'

Figure 2.3 *Don and Harry pose with two denizens of Auckland's Karangahape Road during the* Walkshort *shoot, 1987 (photographer unknown).*

> McGlashan: At the outset I think [director] Bill Toepfer said, 'We can get TVNZ's costume department', so the idea immediately began to grow of the two of us playing lots of different characters; [Sinclair] came back with the script, which had the beginning and the end as a loop … You could lock off a camera and start a new set, and the change would be seamless (that's not the way we did it in the end). [Locking the shot ensures the camera will not move from one cut to another.] That led to the idea of two timeframes that were … happening at the same time.

The characters themselves are also repetitive in the sense of being stereotypes: the jolly, lunching businessmen, the nervous chemist, the tourists, the moonstruck adolescent, the angry atheist. They are all locked into roles that define and limit them. This is also what makes them funny, in line with philosopher Henri Bergson's comment that comedy is 'something mechanical encrusted on the living'.[12] It is the inability to do otherwise that excites laughter in human society, which normally defines living as the ability to adapt to novelty. Laughter is a corrective to rigidity, the inability to adapt. Another kind of circularity is found in music, which often plays with linear time via patterns of repetition and difference. The soundtrack of *Walkshort* (by McGlashan and Wayne Laird of From Scratch) is a type of *musique concrète* made up of repeated traffic noise and the sound of walking. 'Each character has his own footstep "sound". The tourist has squeaky sandshoes. The depressed character has leaden boots, the fraught chemist has a limp.'[13] The rhythms of urban life and the creation of music out of repeating fragments of sound are characteristic of classical minimalism as in the work of Steve Reich or From Scratch. The circular narrative device crops up again in the group's next short film, *The Lounge Bar*, which is discussed later in conjunction with the song which forms its soundtrack, 'Theme from "The Lounge Bar"'.[14] *Walkshort* debuted on TV One on 15 May 1987 as part of the arts programme, *Kaleidoscope*, preceded by an eight minute 'off the wall' introduction to the group, which can be found on YouTube.[15]

There was also the question of finding a record label. They had sent demos of the album to several UK labels, including Beggars Banquet and London Records, 'but they all (politely) passed on it. I think the London Records guy said: "I like 'Andy', but we're a singles label".[16] They decided to look for a local label. They were making enough from touring to put aside money to record – including paying Wellington group Six Volts for recording and rehearsal – so they only needed a pressing and distribution deal, which came about via Annabel Carr at Virgin Records (NZ). Malcolm Black [entertainment lawyer, former singer of

Netherworld Dancing Toys, died in 2019] helped with the legal end of things, as he did at the beginning of the Mutton Birds.

> McGlashan: Grant Campbell, who managed us at the time, came from the film world. He didn't know much about the music industry, but he learned fast, certainly enough to see that a normal 'artist' deal was heavily weighted in favour of the label, and if you could afford to make your own record, you were better off with a pressing and distribution deal. In the end, the Virgin NZ team did more to help publicize us than they really ought to have, given that they weren't making anything like what they'd make if it was a normal 'artist' deal – but I think they were just excited to be working with something local. When we won three NZ Music Industry Awards with *Songs From The Front Lawn* [in 1990], they were overjoyed.

In a year dominated by Margaret Urlich and When the Cat's Away (of which Urlich was a member), they won Most Promising Group, Film Soundtrack/Cast Recording, and Top International Performer. Of course, like so many NZ groups, they responded to these honours by promptly breaking up!

NZ music in the 1980s

The Front Lawn, perhaps because of their theatrical background, fell between camps, in terms of different regional music scenes, namely Auckland and Wellington; the mainstream/commercial and indie scenes, and the international major labels and the local independent labels. Auckland was the centre of NZ popular music – the international labels were based there, it had the biggest population and the most venues. Most established acts were descended from

Auckland bands like Th'Dudes (Peter Urlich, Ian Morris, Dave Dobbyn), Hello Sailor (Graham Brazier, Dave McArtney, Harry Lyon) or Split Enz (Neil and Tim Finn, Phil Judd).[17] At the same time, it wasn't a scene that played on its Auckland-ness very much – rather it was regarded as the gateway to international success – its outlook, so it liked to imagine, was cosmopolitan. Even back in the early 1980s, when a number of indie labels came out of Auckland, like Propeller, they set their sights very high, spending a lot of money on debut albums by Blam Blam Blam and the Screaming Meemees – presumably because they had international markets in mind. When the albums failed to recoup costs, Propeller found itself in trouble.[18] Auckland was quickest to respond to overseas trends, producing a series of commercial bands like Penknife Glides, Coconut Rough, Satellite Spies, Car Crash Set and DD Smash, that produced radio hits and dance music, using synthesizers, Midi drums, sequencers, and the latest studio effects. In turn, they were signed to major record labels (all based in Auckland) and often recorded at Mandrill Studios. The Front Lawn, although certainly interested in new studio technology, took a more home-spun approach, playing on their local-ness – their album cover featured Rangitoto Island in the background, and on the back cover of the CD they posed in front of an Auckland road sign.

This was part of The Front Lawn aesthetic, which was to identify (albeit ironically) with suburbia, rather than pretending, as most rock bands do, that they were from somewhere else (Māori/Pasifika groups also embraced local identity, and with group names like Aotearoa, the Otara Millionaires Club [OMC] and Southside of Bombay, their local roots were fairly clear).

Wellington did not have the same track record of producing hits at the time – seen as a civil servant town, it

Figure 2.4 *On the Northern motorway, North Shore. From LP cover shoot, 1989.*

was generally more focused on high culture, like theatre and classical music. That said, New Zealand's biggest local hit in 1988 was from Wellington group the Holidaymakers, a cover of Bill Withers's 'Sweet Lovers'. The first NZ hip hop group, Upper Hutt Posse, emerged from the Wellington area in 1988, with 'E Tu', on Wellington indie Jayrem, which had also released New Zealand's first electronic hit single, 'Pulsing' by The Body Electric, back in 1983. Wellington was also known for light-hearted, broadly R&B-influenced acts like Bill Lake, the Pelicans, and the Hulamen, most of whom were released by Jayrem, which, unlike most NZ indies, did not have a house style. Finally, there was also the 'Braille cooperative'/Primitive Art Group/ Six Volts axis, which intersected with the Wellington theatre scene, and produced music that ranged from Weimar cabaret to arty noise. They must have been fairly free improvisers, as in a 1989 interview, Sinclair recalls playing with 'those people in Wellington about ten years ago. They've continued in that direction, whereas … I realized I couldn't play the clarinet very well'.[19] David Long (Six Volts guitarist) says, 'The free improv that the Primitive Art Group was doing was probably the most Wellington sound … I dunno whether there was a Wellington rock sound; I saw myself as the generation after, say, Bill Lake and the Hulamen … who were very much into the New Orleans, second line stuff'.[20] *The Hills Are Alive* (Jayrem 1990), the Six Volts' debut album, recorded at Wellington's Marmalade Studios at about the same time as The Front Lawn album, mixed originals with eccentric covers of pop and rock songs like 'Something Stupid' (Frank and Nancy Sinatra) and 'Black Dog' (Led Zeppelin), jazz pieces like 'Caravan' (Duke Ellington) and musical numbers like 'Surabaya Johnny' (Bertolt Brecht/ Kurt Weill). Some saw The Front Lawn/Six Volts collaboration as an unlikely alliance: 'Auckland and Wellington, two cities who [*sic*] … are supposed to be the deadliest of enemies … have actually come together … Music has bridged the chasm of spite and jealousy'.[21]

Recording at Mandrill Studios apparently placed The Front Lawn in the major league, and the group's popularity attracted the attention of major labels, though the deal they signed was for distribution of their own indie, Front Lawn Records. Auckland had many indie labels (from Trevor Reekie's Pagan, another fairly eclectic label, to Warrior Records, which released Māori/Pasifika reggae bands like Herbs), which had grown in the aftermath of punk. While many of the above indie labels flirted with alternative music, Flying Nun Records was the leader. Originally based in Christchurch/Ōtautahi in the South Island, by 1987 it had moved to Auckland. It was allied with the other powerful player in the Auckland alternative scene, University of Auckland student radio station BFM. Run by Debbi Gibbs (daughter of prominent NZ businessman Alan Gibbs) and also in alliance with Doug Hood's Livesound, which hired PAs, and associated touring company Looney Tours, BFM pretty much defined alternative music in Auckland, and the whole country to a degree. That The Front Lawn managed to operate between the indie/ alternative scene and the mainstream speaks to the rather different kind of audience they had through theatre, film and TV, rather than radio. Although student radio did play the group, its trajectory was towards grunge and noise, electronica and hip hop. Increasingly alternative music was marking out its difference from mainstream music, stylistically and culturally, summed up in BFM's slogan: 'Other radio stations are shit.'

The 1980s marked a local popular music renaissance, with a significant rise in the number of local artists writing their own songs, forming bands and releasing records with local independent record labels, a development that can largely be attributed to the influence of punk and its DIY ethic.[22] 'New Zealand music' in this period became a market category, a section in the local record store, often associated with an 'alternative sensibility' – amateur, low-budget, non-commercial, not to all tastes perhaps, but definitely a presence. Flying Nun Records on the one hand and The Front Lawn on the other became, at least to some (both here and overseas), a manifestation of 'New Zealandness'.

Making the album

The recording at Mandrill Studios in Auckland in the summer of 1988–9 was not the duo's first attempt at an album. McGlashan says:

> We made the [album] about three times … We went into Mascot Studios [Auckland] to … recreate the live show,[23] with just electric guitar, two voices and Harry on the squeezebox and some foot stamps, and it sounded really bare and empty. Then we bought [an Akai] 12-track recorder, and installed it in Wayne Laird's studio (in downtown Auckland). The second one we made was more folky, more lush and sentimental 'cos it was pretty much Harry playing the squeezebox and me adding layers of other things.

Eventually they decided they needed a band to realize the songs properly, a process that began in late 1987, in Melbourne, when Chris Gough of Mana Publishing offered to pay for them to demo a song there. McGlashan recalls how they wrote 'A Man and A Woman' 'on the spot' and:

> made quite a rocky demo … because we were driving round Melbourne with Paul Kelly's *Gossip* stuck in the tape player, so we thought … [of making] an album that is not like us on stage at all, it's like a band, and then somebody had the idea we should get the Six Volts.

Six Volts also bridged the gap between music and theatre, being accustomed to performing the former in the latter. David Long says: 'When [we] … started … we were the band for *The Threepenny Opera* [by Brecht and Weill] … at Downstage Theatre [Wellington, 1988] … so we'd worked with Jennifer and Michael Hurst … I don't know whether

Don and Harry saw that, but perhaps that's how we got on their musical radar; we already knew Jennifer'. McGlashan wanted to get the ambience of live performance on the recording: 'When we were onstage, we were dragging in all these characters … even though there's only two of us … but when we listened back [to the initial album recordings] … it just sounded very empty and we thought maybe the Six Volts could bring things to life.'

Long was already a fan:

> When I was 15, one of my favourite bands was Blam Blam Blam … I would sneak into pubs and see them … I'd seen Don doing From Scratch and playing with Ivan Zagni and I'd seen *The Reason for Breakfast*. I loved them but I didn't see the connection to what we were doing. I was surprised when they approached us, except I suppose they were theatrical, and we were theatrical. They [The Front Lawn] obviously wanted … players who weren't … a straight rock band … Six Volts were sort of half jazz players … I was in the less jazz half … Janet [Roddick] came from a classical background … Steve [Roche] played in rock bands … The others [Anthony Donaldson, David Donaldson, Neill Duncan] were in the Primitive Art Group … [Duncan also played sax for Wellington group the Spines, who are still going today].

Long saw groups like Six Volts and The Front Lawn as operating outside or between fields like jazz and rock: 'I didn't wanna be a jazz player, though I was still interested in improv-y groups. I was really influenced by Talking Heads, Adrian Belew, Marc Ribot, Duke Ellington … a lot of world music'. Broadly, his 'aesthetic was post-punk, against the whole macho thing of [blues-based guitar virtuosity] … I had only played really in one rock band [The Tin Syndrome]'.

Figure 2.5 *With the Six Volts, from left (standing): Janet Roddick, Steve Roche, Anthony Donaldson, Neill Duncan; David Long, David Donaldson; The Front Lawn (kneeling); outtake from album cover shoot, 1989.*

At this time, The Front Lawn was also integrating a new member, actor Jennifer Ward-Lealand:

> Don and his first wife Marianne were living next door to us [Jennifer and her partner Michael Hurst] … we were flatting in Parnell [Auckland] … I think that's when they first approached me[24] … And then I guess it was … inevitable that if we were rehearsing for the show [*The One That Got Away*] then we'd help with the album … we had a few sessions where we just threw ideas around, musical ideas [for the show].[25]

These included Jennifer playing bass onstage: 'We [Michael and Jennifer] had booked a holiday in Fiji … and so I took … this enormous guitar case … [and] diligently practiced … in the fale … We ended up not using the bass … I did bvs [backing vocals] and ukulele on the album … I also did the catering … my first and last catering job.' Ward-Lealand had a strong background in music too, singing (solo) in shows of Irving Berlin, Stephen Sondheim and Rodgers and Hart songs at the Mercury Theatre in Auckland, and starring in Brecht's *Threepenny Opera* in 1988 at Wellington's Downstage Theatre.

McGlashan says The Front Lawn 'went down to Wellington for two or three weeks … to rehearse with the Six Volts; they took the stuff and ran with it, we gave them some arrangement ideas'. Jennifer Ward-Lealand comments: 'It was somewhere near the Thistle Hall (Cuba Street) that we practiced for the album.' Long recalls events from Six Volts' perspective: 'Don came down for a couple of days to play with us … I remember him playing "Andy" … and thinking, hell, this is good. The other thing I remember playing was "How You Doing". Don had demos … he had done the demos using Midi.'

For McGlashan, letting other musicians loose on his songs was a hair-raising process: 'I remember thinking, I wish they weren't being rootsy jazzy all over the place [suggesting an ambivalence about ethnic appropriation], but listening back to it now, I think it was a really good idea because you're hearing a bunch of characters, Neill Duncan playing wacky saxophone and Janet Roddick playing trombone.' Long confirms:

> The jazz thing wasn't what they wanted, except some of the second-line stuff … on 'I'll Never Have Anything More', and 'How You Doing', the more fun numbers … [but] it was probably less wild than we would do … We [Long and David Donaldson, bass] were probably the ones who played on [the album] the most … There probably was a bit of [influence from] *Graceland*

(especially with the horns and the accordion), because that was huge at the time.

Sinclair adds: 'I think the Six Volts was a brilliant idea. On my favourite things on the album, "Tomorrow Night," "Andy" and "I'll Never Have Anything More," the Six Volts really humanize what we were doing and gave some of the presence we had on stage to the recording.'

McGlashan contrasts the demos with the recording:

If you take the song 'Andy' ... the way I did it before was mandolin, acoustic guitar, squeezebox, it was very sad and sentimental. With Six Volts, it's more like a fairground, and it cuts against the sadness of the song ... They stopped us overcooking things. They certainly came to it with a lot of thought ... they were a super-democratic group, they would argue about everything they did, every note; they brought that kind of rigour to our recording.

Sinclair has a slightly different view: 'I think they also brought a sort of slight sloppiness, a kind of swing that you [McGlashan] almost resented! You were sort of rigorous [McGlashan laughs]. "Tomorrow Night" ... swings, the things they did with the brass, were really fantastic ... By letting the Six Volts' influence in, we made a much more lasting thing.'

At the same time, a click track was used to record basic tracks. McGlashan says:

We were ... making a pop or rock record and Six Volts was ... a jazz band ... Anthony [Donaldson] was an amazing colourist drummer, and I think of all of them he had the biggest hill to climb ... he's an amazing rock drummer now.[26] He ... was quite

cross with himself for not being able to get some of the feels
… and there are one or two songs where I ended up playing
drums, like 'Claude Rains'.

Long states, 'The songs that I really love … "Andy", "Claude
Rains", "A Man and A Woman" and "Walk Around The
House" … they're actually the straightest songs.' These are
also the songs that pointed towards the Mutton Birds, the
guitar pop/rock group McGlashan and Long would form in
1991, whose musical style fits broadly into the indie guitar
genre.[27]

For Sinclair, recording highlighted the demarcation of roles
within the group:

> When we were doing things in the theatre, it was sort of
> more my world and when we were in the studio, I always
> felt I was in Don's world; I knew nothing about recording …
> Don was doing most of the work, I played the concertina …
> but I didn't particularly like playing it, I learnt enough to just
> barely get through the song, I really had a hard time with that
> concertina!

Long concurs about the different roles: 'Don was quite savvy
technically … There was a bit of a vocal of Harry's that was a bit
out of tune and Don recorded it into a little sampler and then
he used the pitch knob to get it into tune … it was the first
time I had ever seen that done.'

For Long, the recording was a key event in his career, leading
to greater things:

> I was only 23. It was exciting to spend two weeks in a recording
> studio – I hadn't done much recording, and it was always
> with engineers who said, 'Do you want your guitar to sound

like that?' so I was always freaked out, and I think [recording at Mandrill] gave me some confidence … Don and Harry were really keen and it was a really good experience … It was after that that Don and I started talking about a rock band … I was using more distortion, and I was starting to use feedback, and you sort of need to be noisier to explore that.

3 The album

When You Come Back Home

The first song on the album, 'When You Come Back Home', has an obviously welcoming sentiment: 'When you come back home, and you find me waiting there.' It addresses recurring themes of localness, domesticity and gender negotiation. It was also the single, and a video was made.[1] The song leads off with what could be described as a Māori strum, though McGlashan demurs somewhat: 'I guess so, we didn't mean it.'[2] I think this comment hints at the complex politics of ethnic appropriation – Pākehā becoming self-conscious about borrowing from Māori. At the same time, it needs to be acknowledged that ethnic music is the foundation of modern popular music, and a lot of the spirit of the album derives from indigenous and/or imported Black Atlantic influences, the 'rootsy/jazzy-ness' that McGlashan acknowledged feeling slightly queasy about.[3] Michael Brown notes:[4]

> [T]he Māori strum was the most popular manifestation of an entire accompaniment style … it has been given dozens of colloquial names over the years, including onomatopoeic terms like jingajik, dumdejak, and jungajuka, along with English-language expressions like the party strum, the Kiwi strum, and the fish 'n' chip strum … the names provide multiple recognition of the style's existence, and signify its wide diffusion among Māori people and the New Zealand population. They also testify to a stylistic history stretching

back to at least 1940: the Māori strumming style is probably the most enduring and popular guitar style to have yet emerged in New Zealand. In recent years, too, music critics and writers have begun to identify examples of this style – mostly calling them the Māori strum – in recordings by various popular groups from New Zealand, including Split Enz,[5] Hello Sailor,[6] Crowded House,[7] and OMC.[8] As Sally Bodkin-Allen suggests, – the so-called Māori strum 'has become a distinctive sound associated with New Zealand.'[9]

The strum is not just a rhythmic approach, but it also connotes 'certain altered chords (also widely used around the world). Major-sixths and dominant-ninths were apparently typical – party chords'.[10] The first chord of the song is a C# major sixth, and McGlashan and Sinclair repeatedly refer to how Six Volts 'lend themselves to sounding like a party'.

The song also reverses gender roles – sung by men, it suggests that it is the woman who is coming home, to a party (an idea repeated in 'Tomorrow Night'). In the latter song, the 'home' referred to is also a national home, New Zealand, and this connotation also attaches to the Māori strum at the start of the song. Effectively the intro says, 'Welcome to New Zealand!' ('Nau mai ki Aotearoa!'). In this light it is not surprising that the album became a symbol of 'home' for New Zealanders overseas, McGlashan commenting, 'I'm really proud that the album became the one that Kiwis took overseas, that eventually broke in their Kombi as they drove through Prague.' Sinclair concurs, 'It's amazing the number of people who have told me how much the album meant to them when they were living overseas.'

However, the symbolization of New Zealand is subtly different from the traditional iconography of the Kiwi bloke, who is typically an outdoor type. Instead, masculinity is associated with everyday, domestic interiors (an idea also developed in 'Walk Around the House'):

> McGlashan: I guess it's folk music which is about the quotidien … [whereas rock] music is about extremes. I didn't know what kind of music I wanted to write with the Blams and I thought I'd found a voice, but then the band finished and I didn't know what to do with that energy … and with the kind of role and the combination of looking at the world on an angle, the way Laurie Anderson did, and the simplicity and everyday detail of the Irish folk songs I was listening to, [like] Paul Brady and Andy Irvine. This is when I was living in New York, also I was listening to a lot of … country songs where they stopped being country and started being about the suburbs – George Jones talking about what a good year for the roses, I was moving that way.

The song's genesis was a mixed bag of collaboration and circumstance:

> McGlashan: I'd written the bones of it, up to the chorus, for a stage show. I was an artist in residence at a school [Birkdale College, Auckland],[11] and we had this stage musical called Kate and the Flying Bus, about a kid who was ostracized at school and she gets on a bus and everything goes magical, and there were some good lines in that: 'When they all want to turn you down, like the sound on your TV set', and then Harry came up with the big chorus.

> Sinclair: Did I? I can't remember that.

> McGlashan: There were many ways for [ideas] to grow into songs; there was never the normal thing of someone brings the music, someone brings the lyrics … that one was a hybrid, I brought the guts of it, then we finished it together.

The catchiness of the song marked it as a single, but this gave rise to its own problems, according to McGlashan:

> I never thought we got 'When You Come Back Home' … swinging right [on the recording], but … when you decide that something's going to be a single, you tend to, or I tend to … get very tense about it. I'm better these days … It just never really cooked for me; Bruce Lynch [producer at Mandrill Studios] … changed the bottom end a little bit, and it was better, and it gets better as the song goes along, about halfway through it starts to relax. The thing about singles is that it can't be overwrought … You listen to a song like 'Walk Around The House' and it's really sensuous and swingy and it works really beautifully, because we weren't pushing it to be a single.

The single reached number 49 in the NZ singles chart in May 1989, which was not a success. It fell in the cracks as far as NZ radio programmers were concerned, being too alternative for mainstream stations, and possibly too commercial for student radio. Contemporary reviewers echoed this confusion: 'Is it a film? Is it a skit? Is it a love song?' asked the *Auckland Star*'s Russell Baillie (4 May 1989). Baillie commented further that the single sounded under-produced, a comment echoed in other quarters (McGlashan is himself critical of the sound).[12] Indeed, contemporary reviews of the album often sounded a quizzical note, Nick Bollinger opining, 'There's a word I hear every time anyone tries to describe a performance by the Front Lawn: clever. It's a word that has followed Don McGlashan around since way back in the Whizz Kids' [although McGlashan's involvement in that band, which shared members with The Plague, seems to have been very temporary]. 'Fortunately', he continues, 'there is substance beneath the smartness'.[13] Journalistic scepticism combined with overtones of NZ anti-intellectualism and tall poppy syndrome, to suggest that The

Front Lawn didn't quite fit, especially into the genre of rock, an idea made explicit in other reviews: 'This LP makes me want to see the show, and discover if [it] throws these ten songs into context. Until then, I'll pass on this rather pointless collection'; 'this isn't an album of rock music'.[14] Retrospective evaluations tend to be more forgiving, however. In 2009, Bollinger described the album as 'one of the most enduring and identifiably New Zealand collections of song'.[15]

Theme from 'The Lounge Bar'

'Strange how potent cheap music is' – Noel Coward, *Private Lives*.

'We were working on the film [*The Lounge Bar*] and one day Don turned up with the whole song … I loved it', says Sinclair. However, it was never performed live, says McGlashan: 'After the film we went straight on to do other shows like *The Washing Machine* and *The One That Got Away* that had their own songs, so we never had time for it.' As with the shows, in the film, music and drama are intertwined, the song setting the scene for the narrative, both of which shift between past and present to tell the story of a man with amnesia and a brace on his head, drinking in a bar (Sinclair) and his interactions with the barman/singer (McGlashan) and a woman customer (Lucy Sheehan), who has also worked at the bar in the past. The pub setting and kitsch allusions, 'Live a little! It's 1972!', suggest Kiwiana, the same nostalgic local stereotypes sent up in the video of 'There is No Depression in New Zealand'.[16] Kiwiana is an [ironic] assertion of local-ness through nostalgic appropriation of overseas mass culture (processed food like tomato sauce, cheap clothing like 'stubbies' [shorts], plastic jandals and gumboots), also described as Antipodean camp.[17] Essentially, it links identity with nostalgia, very apt in a film about a man who has lost his memory, but also relevant to Pākehā New Zealand, where identity was much easier (and more comfortable) to talk about in the past tense:

> Sinclair: With *The Lounge Bar*, we talked a lot about nostalgia and 'Ten Guitars' [originally recorded by Engelbert Humperdinck in 1967, but now regarded as Kiwiana], and the idea of a chord change [signalling a change in time] and memory … and how multiple time frames seem to be existing at the same time, as we live in our memories, and the film was all about forgetting, and being in the same place at the same time.

McGlashan's take on the film's evolution also emphasizes the role of time:

> The film was scripted very precisely because someone at the Film Commission had discovered that short films of precisely 12 minutes could be used … by some English channel [Channel Four] to fill in the gap at the end of an hour when you had an ad-free day. They were called bonsai features, a whole bunch of Kiwis got funding. I think we were the first.

The track, a pastiche of cheesy 1960s easy-listening *bossa nova*, *à la* Burt Bacharach and Astrud Gilberto, plays a number of tricks on the listener, the first being the melodic leap at the end of the first line: 'There's a man at the bar staring into *space*', which imparts the giddiness of a man falling off his bar stool. Sinclair says: 'I think that Don wrote that song to make sure that I absolutely could not sing it; there is one note that totally escapes me.' But this unexpected note has several functions, startling the listener out of his drunken torpor (given the bar setting), adding a note of parody, and anticipating the surprising twist in the narrative: 'What's that thing on his head? Must have had quite a fall.' The incongruity of the sentiment is underlined by the irregular structure – two nine-bar phrases, followed by a 5 1/2 bar phrase on the line: 'And the song sounds like The Girl from Ipanema.' One possible reason for the irregular bar lengths is that the song is a tool to tell the story – the singer is the narrator – so the phrase lengths change according to the amount of exposition needed. However, the recurring skip or half bar that falls on the word 'Ipanema' highlights that the 1960s lounge classic is literally invading another song, and that another duration or time is present. It could also suggest déjà vu – the hoped-for recognition by the character in the song who has lost his memory after a fall. Music is a powerful aide-memoire because unlike most other media it is not primarily visual, so it registers pervasively as atmosphere rather than as discrete objects.

The rhythm track is a one-bar loop similar to the bossa nova setting on the kind of organ nostalgically associated with lounge acts. McGlashan says:

> It's either a drum machine off a Lowrey Teenie Genie (organ) or a copy off a (Roland TR-606) Drumatix drum machine … we sampled each note into an emulator and that meant we could slightly vary it to the speed of the film, cos we didn't have ProTools in those days – we were working with video that was time-coded, it was a bleedin' nightmare … I quite like how wonky it is.

The half-bars mean that the rhythm track is inverted on occasion (in the sense of starting on the wrong beat). All these rhythmic and metrical tricks add unsettling undercurrents to the song's placid, gauzy surface.

The song also changes key regularly, and besides disorienting the listener, this also achieves specific effects such as on the line, 'But just then a chord-change', which coincides with a key change (from C major to Eb major), a well-worn Tin Pan Alley device for imparting an emotional lift, still common in 1960s pop (the Beatles used it a lot, especially for middle eights, 'You're Gonna Lose That Girl', for example). However, the key abruptly changes again (down a semitone to D major) on the line 'And her heart sings dance, dance to my ten guitars.' As with the half-bar above, the key change signals a temporary usurpation of the music by the Kiwiana of 'Ten Guitars'. But in other respects, the key changes seem unmotivated (e.g. from D major to C major for the solo), as if the track was playing on a faulty jukebox (which it is). In terms of the narrative, the vague 'And the song sounds like la la la' suggests the character trying to place the tune, culminating in the (false?) recognition, 'the song sounds like Ten Guitars'. This chorus formula: 'The song sounds like … ' repeats in D major, then feints towards E major, bringing the track to an irresolute end.

Although the song is full of surprises, it is also highly circular, echoing the narrative, most obviously in the repeated 'and the song sounds like … ', creating an infinite regression of songs about songs that sound like other songs, a befuddlement that echoes the mind of a drinker, or someone with a brain injury. Déjà vu or false recognition of the past in the present can be a symptom of senility, or melancholia.

These themes recur with variations in the final short film made by the group, *Linda's Body* (directed by Harry Sinclair, 1990).[18] The narrative, rather than being circular, is more like *Rashomon* (Akira Kurosawa 1950) in that it is recounted from two different viewpoints, that of the living and the dead, although this is similar to *The Lounge Bar*'s being set simultaneously in the past and present.

In both *Linda's Body* and *The Lounge Bar,* music is linked to nostalgia, melancholy and mourning. In *The Lounge Bar*, the jukebox reproduces in the present a memory of the original live performance. It also stands in for the plight of its invalid protagonist. In *Linda's Body*, the musical leitmotif motivates the key event – the departure of Linda (Jennifer Ward-Lealand) from her body, which literalizes her melancholic wish to be reunited with her dead boyfriend, the singer Victor (Harry Sinclair). If evocation is a quality of music in general, rather than any particular music, potentially any piece of music could do the same job. Accordingly, music in both these films is protean – it changes according to perspective. In *The Lounge Bar*, we have the dual renditions of the theme song as a live performance and as a recording, the characters' commentaries on the song and then the way the song itself alludes to other, similar songs – 'The Girl from Ipanema', 'Ten Guitars'. 'The man at the bar could be anybody', says the song, and by extension, the song that he is listening to could be any song.

In *Linda's Body*, the identity of the leitmotif, first whistled by Ben (McGlashan), Linda's current boyfriend, is also elusive: after Linda's first (temporary) out-of-body experience, she asks: 'What was that tune you were whistling anyway?' and Ben replies, 'Dunno'. He then hears the same tune being hummed by his neighbour, Rangi, who tells him that the song was a favourite of her deceased husband, Hemi (with the strong implication that the couple are Māori).[19] Rangi then lends Ben the record, although a close-up reveals that the song on the record is 'Haere Mai', by Bill Wolfgramm, a 1955 recording sometimes described as New Zealand's unofficial national anthem, and strongly associated with Māori waiata (song), despite being written by a Jewish Pākehā (Sam Freedman).[20] Nevertheless, when Ben plays the record, we still hear the leitmotif, not 'Haere

Mai'. The leitmotif then makes a third appearance, this time as a song with lyrics, 'And now she's gone', with which Victor torments Ben when the latter thinks Linda has left him. Then at the end of the film, when Linda has given up her death wish and been reunited with Ben, the record is played again, and the original recording of 'Haere Mai' is heard. Thus, in each case, the music seems to shape itself according to the perspective of the characters. Music is a material out of which listeners fashion their identity, a 'technology of the self'.[21]

In terms of semiotics, music is not iconic:[22] it does not usually work primarily by imitation, like, say, a statue of a public figure. While it could be argued that it 'represents' a mood or a feeling, in the films, everyone hears the music in their own way. We cannot overlook the investment of the listener, the cathexis which becomes especially important when powerful emotions are already in play, as in mourning and melancholia. When one is already in a highly emotional state, any music can act as a catalyst for expression. Sigmund Freud argues that melancholia is not so much the desire for a lost object as the desire for an object we never had in the first place. In other words, the desire of desire.[23] What the melancholic hears in music is not past emotion, but the very possibility of feeling any emotion. Slavoj Žižek glosses Freud to the effect that melancholia is not a pathology but constitutive of subjectivity. The desire for lost unity covers over the fact that it never existed: we only imagine we are whole, unified beings. At the social level, this is the function of ideology – to make existence cohere. For example, Žižek discusses anamorphosis – just as tears distort our perception of commonplace objects and make them appear other:

Anamorphosis designates an object whose very material reality is distorted in such a way that a gaze is inscribed into its objective features. A face that looks grotesquely distorted and protracted acquires consistency; a blurred contour, a stain, becomes a clear entity if we look at it from a certain biased standpoint – and is this not one of the succinct formulations of ideology … ?[24]

Music in these films has this protean character, transforming itself according to the perspective of the listener. It is a receptacle into which characters deposit their fantasies. The man at the bar is nostalgic for what never happened, i.e. an innocent past in which he did not sexually harass the barmaid (Ngaire) and was not hit over the head with a bottle. Linda is nostalgic for Victor, but the price of reunification is the loss of the ability to feel, or literally to live. *Linda's Body* enacts a similar nostalgia in relation to New Zealand's colonial past, in which the crimes of colonization are washed away by first the revelation of a spirit world inhabited mainly by Māori, and a rousing rendition of 'Haere Mai', at the film's conclusion: 'everything is ka pai [fine]'. At the same time, music is the stuff of social interaction: finding the identity of the song becomes a quest for the characters in the films, and progressive as well as regressive interpretations are possible. In *Linda's Body*, music initiates cultural interaction, for Ben, at any rate. In *The Lounge Bar*, the 'chord change, that makes the blood change direction' hints at the possibility of utopia. The bar manager (who is also the man at the bar in the present) says to Ngaire, 'What do you think?' (of the music) and for a moment the two characters are united as an audience. Ngaire, a name strongly associated with New Zealand, and with an echo in Te Reo, turns up later in McGlashan's career as the title of a Mutton Birds song.[25] Its titular heroine, like the character in the film, is a free spirit, although the perspective of the film (and the song) is masculine.[26]

How You Doing

Probably the most unusual track on the album, with its mixture of spoken word and comedy, 'How You Doing' links to the stage shows more explicitly than the other tracks.

> McGlashan: 'How You Doing' is the most theatrical thing on the album; it was a dance on stage – we'd come out, shake hands … and as soon as we started the dialogue it became a dance … We used to play around with the idea that in NZ, for white people at any rate, ritual was very submerged, and not encouraged … and we … imagined a fictitious place where two guys would meet each other in the street and then go into a dance … It's like Steve Reich, all you have to do to make a piece of speech into music is just repeat it.

'How You Doing' was also about NZ masculinity, with its emphasis on physical, rather than verbal, expression:

> Sinclair: I think it was a lot to do with deconstruction, we were pulling apart ordinary speech, turning it into rhythmic blocks, and we were pulling apart movement, making dance pieces out of guys hammering wood … It was about how we live in NZ: 'This is how NZ men are.' Let's pull apart these pieces and make them into ritualistic performances that help us understand ourselves … these are the building blocks of who we are, how we speak, how we move.

> McGlashan: The [dance] piece Harry is talking about … we had a square of 4x2s [pieces of wood] on the stage, and a hammer in each hand, and we just bashed 'em in rhythm, and every so often we'd stop and say to each other, 'D'you wanna a hand with that?' with all the sense of veiled threat which occurs when two men are working together.

Sinclair: And there was, 'What about a cup of tea?' which we would shout to an imagined woman who was … in the kitchen. We stopped performing [the sketch] when one of the heads of the hammers flew off into the audience. Didn't hit anyone, fortunately.

McGlashan: ['How You Doing'] was begun with the idea that there's a thin line between sanity and madness; if you meet somebody and you reach into your bag of responses and you get the wrong one ['What d'you say to me?'].

Perhaps because it was basically a skit, it proved difficult to render as a piece of music.

McGlashan: In the studio it sounded flat and that's where the Six Volts were really cool, we talked about a sound that was totally not NZ, like something from an Arabian bazaar, totally anti-Kiwi, and they just ran with it, they did a beautiful job … we had to find a way to translate what we were doing onstage to the record.

Long: There was an 8 or 16-bar section [in the song] and Don said, 'Can you do an acoustic guitar solo on that?' and I did something, and Don said, 'Yeah, that's great, now can you double that an octave down?' and I remember going, 'What? – I just improvised it.' And having to sit there and work out what I'd done.

The group's songs often use Kiwi vernacular, for example the substitution of 'a man' for 'I', a device also used by NZ writer Frank Sargeson: 'A man wants a mate that won't let him down';[27] 'A man gets angry, but what can he do?' ('Andy'). 'How You Doing' is based on male–male conversation, but is less a dialogue than a succession of non sequiturs:

A&B: Ah, how you doing, I haven't seen you for …

A: Yes it's quite a while, isn't it?

B: What are you up to these days?

A: Oh keeping busy, how 'bout you?

A: Oh yeh

B: Kevin, isn't it?

A: (Threateningly) What d'you call me?

B: Kevin

A: Kevin, isn't it?

B: Yeh

A: Yeh

B: Hee hee

A: John

B: Mike

A: Mike!

A&B: Ha ha!

A&B: Ah, how you doing, I haven't seen you for …

This gnomic style plays ironically on Pākehā male inarticulacy: compare it with dialogue from Sargeson's 'That Summer':

You fix things, he said.

I'll have a try, I said, but have you got any chips? [money]

No, he said.

Never mind, I said, I'll fix things.

So you got off all right, he said.

How did you work it Terry? I said.

I worked it, he said, and he wouldn't say anything more.

Forget it, he said.[28]

Similar techniques occur in both, like mirroring repetition (where one speaker mirrors the other's expressions), as in the following sequence ('How You Doing'):

A – Hehe, nah

B – Yeah … eh?

A – Hehe, nah

B – Yeah … eh?

A – Hehe, nah

B – Yeah … eh?

The 'Yeah Nah' discourse is now recognized as a feature of Antipodean English. According to one study, 'Yeah-no in Australian English is a relatively new marker which serves a number of functions, including discourse cohesion, the pragmatic functions of hedging and face-saving, and assent and dissent.'[29]

The other local linguistic marker in this example is the New Zealand 'eh?' The 'eh?' has a rising inflection which suggests (without necessarily being) a question, which is common in NZ English, and suggests a strong desire for agreement. According to Miriam Meyerhoff, a professor of linguistics at Victoria University of Wellington, the word is a 'validation checker'.[30] All these devices are phatic, that is, they are about establishing common ground, rather than communicating information. Broadly, they could suggest a culture in which agreement is more important than new ideas (which could cause dissent) and this could connect to the NZ 'tall poppy syndrome' which punishes non-conformity. The comic, tic-like repetitions of 'How You Doing' make fun of the NZ tendency towards agreement at any cost. The phatic functions of language predominate over the expressive. They also suggest unconscious ritual, in a culture that claims to be anti-ritualistic. Unconscious ritual connects to comedy, which is often based on characters that repeat themselves, suggesting catchphrases like Fred Dagg's 'She'll be right' and 'Kick it in the guts, Trev', and *bro'Town*'s 'Not even, ow!' At the same time, the style is cryptic, minimalist and laconic in what could be described as a masculine manner.

Walk Around the House

The song was (probably) written in Islington Street in Herne Bay, Auckland, where Harry Sinclair was living with his girlfriend in the late 1980s. According to McGlashan, the flat was 'right next to a dilapidated Buffalo hall,[31] because late at night, Harry would hear the Buffalos charging, they were a bit looser than Freemasons, they'd sing songs, then they all gather at one end of the hall and charge from one end to the other, with their heads down … that informed some of our thinking about ritual'. Later, in early 1989, the group rehearsed in the Buffalo hall, for *The One That Got Away*.

The recording highlights a different voice, a gentler, more hesitant voice, that of Harry Sinclair. The amount of vibrato he uses gives his singing a nervous but intimate, almost rapt quality, quite unlike McGlashan, a more conventionally accomplished singer and musician. But collaboration brought out the best in both. Sinclair says: 'What we've become really good at is saying no to each other's ideas and not feeling bad about it … I've even started to express ideas that I initially think are really bad, just in case Don says they're really good'.[32] He continues: 'I can't really play any instrument, I don't write songs [that way]. The wonderful thing about working with Don … I would have a little melodic idea and some words that went with it and I was able to bring them to Don and say, "Is there a song in here?"' McGlashan says:

> Harry brought the whole song in and I just put chords to it and wrote a bridge ['Eyes still move when they're closed … '] or something … Because it's about a man standing in a house after dark, it shouldn't have many instruments, or you'd wake everybody up. It grooves along but with quite a light touch … there's a sort of slight ska quality there, no reason for it to be there, but it helps it to cook a bit, and then you've got quite a warm melody with a rhythm that kind of falls over itself. I love that song.

The way the verse melody follows the chord changes could suggest naivety or vulnerability, but also the hesitancy of someone feeling their way around a darkened room. The rhythmic stutter mentioned by McGlashan (a half-bar) occurs on the word 'breathing', so it is literally like someone catching their breath, again suggesting a rapt quality, or possibly a stumble. The substitution of 'sleeping' for 'breathing' nicely conveys the tranquillity of the scene. The half-bar stumble recurs in the bridge (when the line 'Eyes still move …' repeats, so possibly McGlashan picked up on the cue and amplified it).

The song continues the theme of male domesticity. Sinclair says:

> I think we were … trying to construct a new kind of New Zealand man, that was capable of being very loving, and very

The Album

generous to a partner … 'When You Come Back Home', 'Walk Around The House', 'Tell Me What To Do', it was about a kind of sweetness … I had grown up in a culture where that was not really cool.

This is shown in the couplet at the end of the first verse: 'That is the person I love/That is the person I say, "I love you" to.' The use of 'person' suggests that conventional gender roles are not important to the speaker (as in 'the woman I love'). And the specification of the last line suggests that loving someone requires work – that love is not a disposition but a performance – it needs to be demonstrated through kind words and actions.

The song also refers to another Front Lawn activity – walking. Walking is part of *Walkshort*, 'Andy' ('Let's take a walk on the beach'), and of course, 'the girl from Ipanema goes walking' ('Theme from "The Lounge Bar"'). Walking is a characteristically domestic mode of transport. You can do it on your front lawn. It is contrasted with 'trudging to work in the dim light' of London ('Tomorrow Night'). It is distinct from flying, driving or even running. Again, it suggests a modesty that sets it apart from the standard rock vocabulary of speed and power – those endless songs about cars, trains, planes and rockets. For Michel De Certeau, 'the "arts of doing" such as walking, talking, reading, dwelling, and cooking', were evidence that 'despite repressive aspects of modern society, there exists an element of creative resistance to these structures enacted by ordinary people'.[33] One only needs to think about the recent controversial proposal to build a walking and cycling bridge over the Waitemata Harbour in Auckland to see that walking is a political activity.[34]

Andy

McGlashan: With 'Andy', I brought pretty much a whole finished song in, but it had a whole bunch of scaffolding about the emptying of the countryside because of Rogernomics … it had two brothers, one was rural, one was urban … it was kind of a grief song, some of it was to do with this country that we've lost, which is now full of carparks and glass towers … and Harry said, 'Well, this is about your brother, isn't it, why don't we just essentialize it?' (McGlashan's elder brother, Alexander/Alec, died at 20 in a boating accident in 1974.)

Sinclair: Entirely Don's song; my role was to help it be more focused.

McGlashan: And also to find out what the point of it was. Sometimes people send me songs and I think, 'What are you really getting at here? There's about three songs here', and that was where 'Andy' got a new life, because Harry basically said, 'If you can write just one song about your brother, maybe we can move forward, and there won't be so much unfocused grief everywhere.'

Sinclair: Really?

McGlashan: You gave me quite a hard time about it, but it was really valuable.

I recall going into a pub in Punakaiki on the West Coast of the South Island in 1983. I asked for a beer and the barman ignored me. My (male) friend pulled me aside and said, 'You have to say "mate".' So I said, 'Can I have a beer, mate?' and the barman served me. Mateship, or friendship between men, is an important theme in New Zealand culture, historically, as the primary expression of Kiwi bloke male sociality.[35] This song can be heard as McGlashan and Sinclair's take on mateship. Acoustic guitar and accordion impart an atmosphere of folksy authenticity and frankness.[36] The situation is a beach, a traditional site of Antipodean recreation and intimacy – the narrative beginning as a slightly irritated but affectionate rebuke: 'You sure missed one hell of a party last night … Yeh I know you didn't mean to let me down.' The entire first verse is sung over a drone, without chordal accompaniment, in a laid-back tone – words not falling on beats, Nick Braae commenting that 'the accompaniment that goes nowhere, rhythmically or harmonically, enacts the narrator's inability to move forward in his life.'[37] The tone is vernacular, the feeling disingenuously casual, but the chorus introduces an uncharacteristically pleading tone: 'Andy, don't keep your distance from me', which raises the question: Why is Andy keeping his distance?

The song proceeds by a series of reminiscences: 'We used to go diving from the rocks over there', leading to the conclusion: 'There's not much left of the place we knew when we were kids.' Thus, the theme of loss is introduced. The middle eight gathers momentum by way of an outburst, ostensibly against modern society, culminating in the lines:

A man gets angry, but what can he do?

I don't know why I'm telling this to you

On Takapuna Beach

The method of the song is that we don't know why the narrator gets upset until the last verse: 'I turned 28 last night, if you were still alive you'd be just short of 33 … Andy, don't keep your distance from me.' The poignancy and irony of 'mateship' turns on the fact that Andy, the narrator's brother, is dead. The method is that of the short story, with the 'punchline' held back to the end. The narrative is structured around a disavowal of love: we only discover the truth at the end of the song, and the narrator's feelings of anger and sadness are projected on to an intermediary object. Such a device is also frequent in NZ literature, in Frank Sargeson's 1940s short stories, 'A Great Day' and 'Sale Day' for example, where it is associated with male indirectness.

Also effectively buried in the song is the literary tradition that enshrined such odes to brotherly love. Bruce Mason's *The End of the Golden Weather* (1960, filmed in 1991), the classic Kiwi reminiscence of (male) childhood friendship is also set on Takapuna Beach, and the beach also has strong associations with local writers – Allen Curnow and Sargeson lived close by. But the song makes it clear that the (literary) past is dead and the narrator is alone: 'There's not much left of the place where we were kids.' Finally, the song also has a gendered political subtext – it is a farewell to the 'big brother' parochialism and economic protectionism of the Muldoon era, as the narrator observes the effects of free market on Auckland: 'They're making money out of money/They're making buildings out of glass/Their kids look like they stepped out of fashion magazines/And none of it's gonna last'.

The creation of this song re-enacts its subject matter. A song about mateship is also enacted in the collaboration between McGlashan and Sinclair. Although McGlashan and Sinclair focus on how the song was refined to remove extraneous material, it works partly because it avoids tackling its subject head on – and in the Auckland skyline, McGlashan finds an 'objective correlative' for his feelings about death. This idea can be more simply understood in terms of the cinematic dictum of showing rather than telling. This is apt because McGlashan especially often writes cinematically, describing a

Figure 3.1 *On Takapuna Beach. Rangitoto Island in background. From LP cover shoot, 1989.*

scene or situation rather than talking about his feelings. And this can further be understood, to some degree, as a masculine approach, that has some precedent in NZ cultural tradition: As novelist Maurice Gee says of Rex Petley, his (fictional) NZ master poet in *Going West*, 'He began, quite simply, with describing … I dealt with what I saw and how I felt about it, and what my feelings meant; Rex with what he saw and what he saw next.'[38] Compared to McGlashan, Sinclair has a more critical take on Kiwi masculinity; perhaps this is why he gave McGlashan a hard time about the song!

Writing a song for theatrical performance implies several things: that people will be listening to the words, so perhaps a higher level of contrivance will be expected; the audience will be more likely to expect a dramatic or role-playing song than they would in a rock context; they would expect to identify on some level with the song and especially the lyrics:

> McGlashan: Songs usually start with fragments of lyrics. Then I fill a few pages with general ideas about the song – what's the mood of the singer and situation – are there songs, stories or films this might turn out like? Then I usually leave it for a while before coming back to look for patterns, choruses and verses. Sometimes the sketch will contain a phrase that … I realise must be the title and when that happens the song usually writes itself pretty quickly. I don't generally start writing the music till I'm pretty far down this path …[39]

Like films, McGlashan songs tend to open with a descriptive scenario, an approach extended in the Mutton Birds, e.g. 'A Thing Well Made' or 'Ngaire':

> The plane touches down
>
> The lounge fills up again
>
> With retired couples from the midwestern USA
>
> They blink in the foreign light
>
> And admire each other's shoes
>
> I've seen a lot of new shoes today.

This neutral, descriptive style is not typical of popular music, which tends to focus on expressions of personal feeling, except for a few more scholarly writers like Randy Newman, Paul Simon or David Byrne. McGlashan shares with them the approach of self-consciously adopting a persona, as opposed to what Byrne has referred to as the 'exaggerated individuality' that is 'the normal point of view … in rock'.[40] But broadly,

McGlashan's writing evolved to become more similar to that of the latter-day Bruce Springsteen, writing 'realistic' stories of ordinary men in a 'classic' rock format, an approach that has in turn been seen to appeal to a left-wing populist literary tradition of protest, especially the works of John Steinbeck.[41]

Finally, it should be noted that the duo was indeed concerned about the demolition of much of Auckland's built heritage in the late 1980s, under the aegis of Rogernomics: 'Every time we return … we see a new part of Auckland destroyed without apparent concern for the needs of the people', said Sinclair in 1988. McGlashan added, 'As performers, it's important to us that public spaces stay intact, but in Auckland it's the public spaces that go first and that's a real tragedy.'[42] These political sentiments influenced the duo's later shows, especially *The Washing Machine*, with its critique of consumerism, and contrasting visions of New Zealand past and present.

Tomorrow Night

In 1980s New Zealand, the cultural cringe was still in full effect: 'We didn't think of New Zealand as having any stories worth telling, or any places worth showing.'[43] Film director Jane Campion noted, 'New Zealand is a country hysterically concerned with playing yourself down.'[44] The makers of local TV soap *Shortland Street*, which first aired in 1992, feared that local audiences would not accept Kiwi accents.[45] This was also true of the music industry, which generally treated local product with suspicion. For example, when ex-Split Enz member Neil Finn's new group Crowded House released their eponymous first album in New Zealand in 1986, it received little radio play and sold modestly. This seemed surprising, as he had recently enjoyed a stream of self-penned hits with Split Enz, such as 'I Got You', 'One Step

Ahead' and 'Message to my Girl'. A few months later, a single, 'Don't Dream It's Over', from the album, reached number two in the US charts. NZ radio stations immediately started playing the song, it became a huge hit, and has been voted number two NZ song of all time by an APRA (Australasian Performing Rights Association) songwriters and musicians' poll in 2002.[46] This pre-eminence came about primarily because the song was a US hit.

Sinclair: We were quite nationalistic. It really bothered us that people didn't want to sing about New Zealand places. We felt we should really sing about New Zealand, about us. We grew up with the colonial cringe. I remember my father would never go to the theatre in New Zealand, only in the West End of London would he dream of going to the theatre.

McGlashan: [But] we never sat down and thought, what's a Kiwi thing to do?

Sinclair: It's amazing the number of people who have told me how much the album meant to them when they were living overseas … particularly 'Tomorrow Night' was an important song for a lot of people.

McGlashan: There are lot of folk songs about heroes and I wanted 'Tomorrow Night' to be about this friend of mine who was heroic because she lived a really vivid life, everybody was really looking forward to her coming back … She was my girlfriend and we were together for a while. I didn't want to write just a love song, I wanted to write something that was bigger and more open … We were in England and we met Tim Finn [Split Enz], he was living in Kennington [South London] with Greta Scacchi and he said 'What are you doing?' and I said we were working towards an album and there's one song I'd really like to get a version of down, and he lent us his studio. Tim's always been a real supporter, Neil

[Finn] too, he really liked 'Andy'. I played that to him before we'd made the album.

Arising from the same source as the cultural cringe was a neurosis about NZ art being derivative, which could also mean that non-local references were forbidden. However, The Front Lawn were happy to break this rule, referring to *Casablanca* in 'Claude Rains', 'The Girl from Ipanema' in 'Theme from "The Lounge Bar"' and 'Skye Boat Song' in 'Tomorrow Night'. McGlashan says:

> In the same way as with 'The Lounge Bar', I was interested in the idea of referencing a song within a song … the idea of a party, everybody's looking forward to someone coming back. There's lots of songs like that: 'The Boys are Back in Town' [Thin Lizzy], 'Eli's Coming' by Laura Nyro … When we depart and when we arrive, we're calling on bigger and older forces.

This comment recalls another, edgier comment McGlashan once made to me on the subject of leaving and returning to New Zealand: 'If you leave you've abandoned us, and if you come back you've failed', a reflection on the Mutton Birds' career and the NZ knocking machine. McGlashan says: '[The song] also gave us a chance to vent some of our anti-UK ideas' ['While people trudged to work in the dim light'], but Sinclair adds: 'That song was also about us in a way; we could've stayed in England, we were offered big things in TV … but we were very determined to return, to make New Zealand the place where we did our work; we wanted to be New Zealanders.'

McGlashan reflects on the fact that a song, or any piece of art, expands in meaning as it disseminates, and that incorporating other songs is a tacit acknowledgement of this process of semiosis:

> Quite often when you make something, you don't know why
> you're making it, you're following it where it wants to go, and
> when you've finished it and you listen to it, you think, well, this
> is actually about this and this and that … We just like to drop
> references in because we thought they were cool. But they also
> make the song bigger, more open.

The reference to 'Skye Boat Song' suggested a Celtic strain that
was to become more prominent in McGlashan's later work.

'Tomorrow Night' also achieves the rare feat of being a
man's song about a woman that does not romanticize or
demonize its subject. Along with 'When You Come Back
Home', the album's most accessible song, it shares similar
themes: celebration, home and a kind of implicit feminism.
Both songs have straightforward structures, chords, melodies
and singable choruses. The song's extended chorus of 'la la
las' seems especially designed for participation, seeming 'to
summon up all [its subject's] feelings of belonging'.[47] Its verse
is based around a basic I IV shuttle, then a pre-chorus section
that goes up to the V dominant chord ('She'd go dancing in
the weekends') but substituting a Vm, or minor, a subtle device
that amplifies the exuberance of the dominant V when it finally
arrives at the start of the chorus, which uses a simple, easy-
to-participate-in cycle of fifths structure (V I IV). The lyrics tell
the story of a young woman from the Hutt Valley, 'looking
for something', who likes to go dancing, first in Wellington
pubs, and then in London nightclubs, on her 'OE' [Overseas
Experience]. This latter phrase, coined by 1970s NZ journalist
Tom Scott, refers to a rite of passage: young New Zealanders'
working holidays in the UK, especially London (and Europe,
when the UK was part of the European Union). It could be
seen as part of 'recolonization', referring to the maintenance of

strong economic and cultural ties with the historic colonizer, a process which could subvert nationalist claims about a distinct NZ identity. David Long: 'The OE thing … You went overseas to London … was so much part of our generation … that was when we'd get the *NME* [in NZ] and it was three months old.' Indeed, the 'Skye Boat Song' quote in the last verse could be heard as dramatizing the tug of the 'mother country'. The accompaniment pauses, suggesting irresolution, before the band strikes up again and McGlashan affirms: 'No she didn't wanna stay there, she's on her flight.'

The instrumentation by Six Volts also courts accessibility, via Paul Simon's *Graceland* (1986), which brought 'world music' (specifically South African sounds of accordions, lap steels and exotic percussion) into popular usage, an appropriation of ethnic musical style heightened by the accusation that Simon had broken a ban on cultural contact with South Africa, which was still ruled by apartheid.[48] There is a difference between pastiching a popular style and quoting it self-consciously. The Front Lawn, in general, were masters of the latter – they celebrated intertextuality, as opposed to imitating something fashionable. However, given recent controversies about playing sport with South Africa, playing music linked to South Africa might have also given the musicians pause. McGlashan had always made his position clear – in 1985, he recorded a single 'Don't Go', which also featured local musicians Chris Knox and Rick Bryant, expressing opposition to a proposed All Blacks (NZ national rugby union team) tour of South Africa.[49] The musical style of this track was also South-African influenced, although in this case there is a clear justification. The tour did not go ahead, although a 'rebel' tour in 1986 did. Apparently there was also an 'answer' record, 'Let Them Go' by the Silent Majority.[50]

Claude Rains

McGlashan: That one had been sitting round for a while. The idea was a song about nuclear war … a topic you can't approach head on … I thought … the idea of looking at a story that's got courage and self-sacrifice, even in a minor role, and then dollying back … and saying, if this backdrop wasn't the Second World War, if it was a nuclear holocaust, none of that courage or self-sacrifice would matter. I heard someone once criticising it, saying the film is so much more fun than the song, that's totally missing the point, the song's not about the film … it is about what happens to our little choices, our smallest everyday acts of bravery, when … people say war brings out the best in us … idiots say that, in my view, and I suppose that is why I wanted to write the song, I wanted to say that those people are fucking idiots. [Claude Rains] does something mildly heroic in the end, by not arresting them – he says, 'Arrest the usual suspects.' [It was] … a crazy big thing to try and write a song about, so I ended up doing what we both quite often do, which is to start off with an idea and then start rubbing it out, and you see what's left.

For a long time I didn't have the chorus, it just went, 'La la la'. I think it was when we were rehearsing with the Six Volts before I got around to writing those chorus words. I wasn't sure at the time if it was carrying too much freight [it started off being a song about nuclear war and it ended up being a song about Claude Rains].

A number of songs on the album examine relationships between men including 'Andy' (about mateship), 'A Man and a Woman', 'How You Doing' and 'Claude Rains'. But these songs avoid 'macho' representations, such as we might expect in, say, hard rock or heavy metal, even when their subjects include war.

In my view, 'Claude Rains' is an investigation of masculinity set in the Second World War, significant to the degree that, according to Harry's father, historian Keith Sinclair, NZ soldiers became 'aware of differences between men from Great Britain and from the several colonies. They came to consider their identity self-consciously'.[51] The song is not about New Zealanders directly, however, refracting its concerns through a meta-fictional device – it's a song about an actor who is playing a character in a film about a war. This device suggests a certain ironic distance from traditional local representations of men in wartime, Gallipoli and the Anzacs for example. It focuses on the actor Claude Rains, whose portrayal of Inspector Renault in the film *Casablanca* [1942] seems an unedifying prospect for rock and roll mythologization or local canonization. Renault is a policeman (in conventional rock terms an object of derision), an authority figure, thoroughly anti-heroic, up to his neck in corruption and decidedly effete. In the film he contrasts with the hero, Rick, played by Humphrey Bogart, the archetypal American tough guy with a heart of gold. In his own way, Bogart tends to portray a masculine ideal, especially in his attempts to be impassive and 'not get involved' (a similar scenario occurs in NZ cinema of unease film *Sleeping Dogs* [1977] where the hero, played by Sam Neill, resists joining the rebels, even though he's being persecuted by the state). In this sense, 'Claude Rains' interprets *Casablanca* as being very much about a subordinate and a dominant masculinity, and there are even homoerotic undercurrents to their relationship in the film, as when Renault says: 'If I were a woman I would be in love with Rick.'

Rains (Renault) is 'a functionary through and through … a small man', sings Don monotonally, in a small solitary voice over two chords of surpassing plainness. The ordinariness of the man is being insisted upon. The song continues:

Claude Rains gave the orders to collect the usual suspects

And the camera came in close up on his face

He watched as the plane left the airstrip

Like hope leaves a dying man

But he hung on to the choice he'd made

There is no close-up of Renault at this point in the film (the finale). McGlashan effectively reverses the film's emphasis on Rick to concentrate on the marginal character of Renault. He's marginal in other ways too: as a representative of the Vichy French administration, he is morally ambiguous and necessarily passive (France had already been defeated) – in terms of the masculine dialectic of war, he is effectively emasculated, his powers severely circumscribed. There are parallels between New Zealand and France in the subordinate relation of both to the United States, in military (France) or cultural terms (New Zealand). Casablanca, a French colony, is an isolated place like New Zealand that everyone wants to leave, and 'America' is the mythical place they all want to go. By choosing to identify with Renault, McGlashan takes the marginal man and makes him central. Implicitly there's a connection between Renault's identity as this 'small man' and concepts of local cultural identity as at once independent and marginal.

By identifying with Renault, McGlashan's song also celebrates a masculinity that is of a piece with earlier male NZ writers, in its 'realistic' concentration on the ordinary man who is incarcerated in a beautiful prison, or, in the terms of John

Dix's rock history of New Zealand, *Stranded in Paradise*. Renault's power is limited – 'a small act of defiance' is all he is permitted, characteristically a negative one: 'he could've tried to stop them' i.e. Bogart and his girlfriend, played by Ingrid Bergman. But he 'hangs in there' – 'he hung on to the choice he'd made', i.e. he remains in Casablanca with Rick. His characterization as a 'functionary' is also suggestive. The implication is paradoxical, as one's 'function' is normally distinct from one's identity, but 'through and through' implies the opposite. Renault is an 'instrument' of an administration he doesn't believe in. He is alienated in a routine of meaningless or morally questionable work, a theme McGlashan returns to in the Mutton Birds' 'A Thing Well Made' and which arguably becomes his inflection of the 'man alone' theme.

Tell Me What to Do

Another song by written and sung by Harry Sinclair, 'Tell Me What to Do' shares with 'Walk Around the House' a hushed atmosphere, an intimate tone, and similar lyrical themes, but the music, while similar in genre, is more irregular and this makes the feeling more tense. The bass sets up a groove in which the accent falls, confusingly, on the fourth beat of the bar (usually it would fall on the first beat). The vocal enters, again confusingly, on the eighth bar (because popular music usually works with even numbers of bars, the norm would be to complete eight bars before coming in). The vocal is also rhythmically off-kilter with the backing track, creating an effect of skittering nervousness. The verse is entirely on one chord, making it similar to 'How You Doing?', with which it shares some spoken, rather than sung, vocal phrases. The vocal melody is based on a blues scale, making it the only song on the album in that mode, and in blues fashion, there is a clash between the melody and the backing, which implies a tonality of E major. The chorus continues this bluesy mode, using the chords G and C major (which fit the melody). The middle eight ('Why don't you tell me?'), actually a middle nine, modulates into D major, a repeated three-bar pattern of D F G major, against a pedal in D. These bluesy changes, combined with the Six Volts avant jazz skronk-ing, and wah-wah guitar, set the song apart from the rest of the album.

Lyrically, the song is similar to 'Walk' insofar as it suggests sensitive masculinity. But it is also more subjective and expressive, which in some ways makes it closer to conventional pop-rock, with its emphasis on personal expression. Combined with a blues mode, this often creates a persona that is powerfully emotional – whether blues braggadocio, or the tragic lament of the wronged lover. In contrast, the persona of this song, is, as the title implies, apparently quite abject. On one level, this persona could fit with Sinclair's intention to re-imagine NZ masculinity as sensitive and un-macho. At the same time, it seems almost too abject – its repeated entreaties start to sound like demands. It fits within the gamut of characters Sinclair plays who are apparently servile but are in fact manipulative, for example the invalid in *The Lounge Bar*, who seems helpless, but has a history of abusive behaviour. Similarly, Victor in *Linda's Body* seems innocent enough until we realize that he wants Linda to kill herself. The evocation of an extreme state of mind, close to madness, seems to relate most obviously to punk and new wave, for example a song like Talking Heads''Psycho Killer'. At the same time, this persona is not particularly threatening – their delusions seem quite impotent. In 1987, the film *Blue Velvet*, directed by David Lynch, linked Roy Orbison's 'In Dreams', a romantic song about a hopeless dreamer, to a psychopath, played by Dennis Hopper. This weird juxtaposition served to highlight how this apparently innocent song could have a sinister new meaning, given that both the song and the film are about delusions. To me, this song captures something of that ambivalence.

A Man and a Woman

> McGlashan: It was a typical Front Lawn write 'cos Harry came up with the chorus, right up to [the line] 'Don't wake them up', and I said, 'Why wouldn't you wake them up?' And Harry said, 'I dunno.' So, we wrote the verses about two guys coming to a bach [holiday home] and seeing a window open, put in the whole adultery theme … Harry came back with the names of the two people he was staying with in Melbourne which was very impolitic.

> Sinclair: They're no longer together; I think it was because of the song (laughs). No.

This song inaugurates two McGlashan tropes: the exotic ballad form he uses sometimes when writing about women; and the Kiwi Gothic (bad things happening in the countryside).[52] An example of the former is 'Anchor Me'. The two songs share slow/medium tempo, spare arrangement, Latin rhythm, warm textures, a syncopated guitar line with tremolo and of course a lyric that involves a woman in a romantic situation. But these are not happy songs – the situation they describe is always perilous in some way, and this seems to relate to the storm of emotions that threaten to surface. This is explicit in 'Anchor Me"s metaphors of tempests and shipwrecks. 'A Man and a Woman' is about the perils of adultery. The song narrative concerns two men, friends of 'Eugene and Sarah', who make an unsolicited visit to the couple's bach.

The song is in a minor key, which is apt, given the sombre theme. The arrangement is very sparse, which also imparts a haunted quality. The central feature is a gentle ukulele strum, played by Jennifer Ward-Lealand; there is also recurring Shadows-style guitar motif, a string bass and a little Latin percussion (claves).

The irregular verse is made up of a repeated five-bar sequence in Bm: Bm D G F# E. It sounds like a four-bar sequence with an extra bar. This literally creates a pause or hesitation, an irregularity which chimes with the narrator's observation, 'That's strange.'

This dislocation of time is compounded when this sequence is repeated, ending in the line, 'You really should meet him', where another two beats is added to the phrase, making it 5½ bars. Again, this creates the effect of an interjection, an effect reinforced by alternating lines being sung by McGlashan and Sinclair, thereby turning the song into a male–male duet. The interjections become literal as the two characters interrupt each other with the imperative 'Look … '

Meanwhile the music proceeds as a series of three 2 ½ bar phrases, with the lines:

Sinclair: Look, there's a window open

McGlashan: Look, there's a curtain blowing

Both: I wonder who left it like that? McGlashan: Wait a minute …

The metrical surprises clearly echo the surprise of the narrators, the reason for which the chorus does not immediately reveal:

A man and a woman

A woman and a man

Look at them lying there

Sleeping in each other's arms

Don't wake them up, leave them sleeping

Don't wake them up

Whereas the verse is tortured and irregular, the chorus appears relatively calm, both metrically and harmonically – the first eight bars stick on the same chord, giving a sense of serenity, reinforced by the melody's simple pentatonic phrases and the repetition/inversion of the title phrase. It seems at first that everything is 'Ka pai' (okay). It's not a burglary, it's just a couple sleeping, so when they sing, 'Don't let them know we've seen them', we imagine that this is simple modesty, but when McGlashan continues 'Don't say a word to anyone', we wonder why, until finally McGlashan reveals all:

'Cos that's Sarah there, that's Eugene's wife, but that's not Eugene …

McGlashan sings these last lines with a keening vibrato quite unlike his usual style. It could almost be described as soulful. Indeed, the song style, a minor key lament with a Latin lilt, recalls 'Gypsy Woman' by the Impressions, a 1960s Chicago soul vocal group led by Curtis Mayfield, another song which features femininity as exotic attraction.

In terms of the gendered narrative, it is notable that the two narrators seem to take the woman's side, 'Sure, Eugene's my friend but he's never going to know.' In a way, their position is like Inspector Renault in *Casablanca* – who decides to do nothing. Though this is a 'small act of defiance' (against the Nazis), it's not clear that this is the case in 'A Man and a Woman'. Rather it is a simple case of letting sleeping dogs lie. This could reflect something about Pākehā society – the conflict avoidance addressed in Bill Pearson's 1952 essay 'Fretful Sleepers' which Gordon McLauchlan extended into a 1976 book, *The Passionless People*.[53] However, this reticence apparently works in Sarah's favour. But it also works in the men's favour as they don't have to risk their friendship with Eugene by telling him the truth.

The other reference in this song is to the Kiwi Gothic – which McGlashan initiated with Blam Blam Blam's 'A Call For Help' (1981), continuing through 'White Valiant' (Mutton Birds 1992) and 'Too Close to the Sun' (Mutton Birds 1994): a sequence of sombre meditations on rural New Zealand, the Antipodean equivalent of 'something nasty in the woodshed',[54] or the hellish hillbillies of *Deliverance* (1971). All these texts have the same theme – the city dweller's fear of the country. In New Zealand, this has an additional, gendered connotation – given that the Kiwi bloke is rural, his taciturnity is a concealed threat (see, for example, the Southern Man Speight's adverts, or virtually any film referenced in Sam Neill's *Cinema of Unease* [1995]). Because the NZ countryside is male territory, women are typically seen as troublesome, which certainly seems to apply here: the song starts with two men, who talk about meeting another man in the countryside, and then an unexpected woman spoils the party.

I'll Never Have Anything More

The sentiments of this Harry Sinclair song certainly make it seem like a fitting end to the album; as does the New Orleans second line, party feel added by Six Volts, combined with a reggae skank from the guitar. Interestingly, in virtually all of Sinclair's tracks, Six Volts have added reggae elements to the backing. There is a relationship between 1950s New Orleans rock and roll, which often rhythmically accented the offbeat, and reggae (or more accurately, its predecessor, ska), which highlighted this element.[55] Radio stations broadcasting from New Orleans could be heard quite clearly in Jamaica. In 1970s UK, reggae shared with punk the title of underground or rebel music, and was a major influence on post-punk, and thereby on 1980s music in general: for example, McGlashan had experimented with reggae on Blam Blam Blam's 'Got To Be Guilty' (1982).

According to Sinclair:

> Those words and that tune came to me … in the 70s when I was living in Wellington and walking down Fairlie Terrace (in Kelburn, near the University) and … hung around in my head for many years … it would have gone nowhere had I not ended up working with Don … My songwriting was just me going for a walk and a little melody would pop into my head.

McGlashan says: 'That's still the way we work, for *Kiri and Lou* (current children's series on TVNZ), we've written nearly 70 songs, some of our best work. Harry will bring a fragment which I finish. Or a whole thing which I then arrange.'[56] He continues: 'Tim Finn said to me, "['I'll Never Have Anything More'] could be a global hit if you just wrote another verse; it could just be [something like] I'll never BE anything more"', says McGlashan. However, the song works as a confirmation of its own lyrical premise – I'll never have anything more than this verse of lyrics. But why would I need another verse? The lyric is about living in the moment and giving up the anxiety of what happens next. For this reason, perhaps, it was often the last song they would perform, on *The One That Got Away* tour, for example. The song sums up an aspect of the group's approach – focus on the small things, on the everyday, and the big picture will take care of itself. One writer opined that "'I'll never have anything more than I've got today" is not a bad philosophy for these greedy times'.[57]

4 The aftermath

The album was released (in New Zealand only) in June 1989,[1] during the group's final NZ tour, for which they travelled in a Pontiac covered in shaggy green material, filming promo clips in NZ towns for weekly appearances on TVNZ show *Radio With Pictures*.[2] 'It was a very creative time … the album, the show, the film (*Linda's Body*), all in 1989. Our team, Grant Campbell [manager], Malcolm Ibell [sound engineer], were a happy little band', says Ward-Lealand.

The show was *The One That Got Away* (more of which below), though it included an encore of 'Andy', 'Tomorrow Night' and 'I'll Never Have Anything More' from the album. Later in August the group travelled to the Edinburgh Festival, their

Figure 4.1 *And then there were three … The Front Lawn in 1989, with Jennifer Ward-Lealand (centre).*

Figure 4.2 *The Front Lawn on tour in New York, 1989. Note the Twin Towers in the background.*

show also being included in a subsequent Pick of the Fringe series in London. Then the group performed in the United States before returning to New Zealand to do a season at the Maidment Theatre, Auckland, in late 1989.

In April 1990 they played at the Melbourne Comedy Festival in Australia, and at the Memorial Theatre, Wellington. But apart from a one-off reunion with The Topp Twins at Auckland's Waterfront Theatre in 1991,[3] that was it. McGlashan says:

> We worked together in this amalgam of theatre and film and music and then at a certain point Harry realized that he was a filmmaker. It took me a bit longer to realize that I didn't want to do these multifarious things – I didn't want to be a Swiss Army knife, I just wanted to be a knife! And my knife was to write songs and that's why I started The Mutton Birds. But that was late in the piece. I was already 29, nearly 30. Most people have worked things out a bit earlier than that.[4]

There didn't seem to be any hard feelings involved: 'We all went off and did different things', says Ward-Lealand. However, in an interview with Gareth Shute, McGlashan went into more detail, reporting that Sinclair had said to him, 'I want to write the next piece [*Linda's Body*] all on my own.' McGlashan continued, 'I played the victim for some time, but it was a bit academic really because by then … I needed a vehicle that was really just all about the songs.'[5]

Nevertheless, there was some unfinished business. In 1993, the group released a second album, *More Songs from The Front Lawn*, also on Front Lawn/Virgin Records, with a single 'The Beautiful Things' and an accompanying music video, directed by Fane Flaws, which won best video at the 1993 New Zealand Music Video Awards.[6] The album charted at number 15 and the single at number 22, both higher positions than achieved by the first album and single in 1989. Despite this, the album quickly dropped from sight, because the group was no longer performing, thus promotion was lacking. It featured songs from Front Lawn shows from the 1987–9 period – unlike the first album, each song was connected to a particular show. 'Possibly, the first album you could enjoy [even] if you didn't know anything about The Front Lawn, [while] the second album is more a record of songs from theatre shows', says McGlashan. 'We wanted the record to be a celebration of our live work, which has really come to an end now', commented Sinclair.[7] The album was home-recorded, presumably on the Akai 12-track, and has a much more contemporary electronic sound than the first album, with sequenced drums, more keyboards and more prominent studio effects. Connectedly, this album did not feature a band – it was mostly the duo, with some help from technology. As with the first album, Graeme Myhre engineered.

Opening track 'The Big Room' also opened The Front Lawn Monster World tour in 1988–9. As its name implies, it is addressed to the performing space itself and the people in it – both performers and audience. With lines like 'Some of us put on trousers, some put on perfume, but we're all in the same room', the track follows the group's philosophy 'that the audience should be the director, and the reactions of the crowd dictate[d] … the show'.[8] The snare drum is a bit loud, however.

'Found Another Body' is a Harry Sinclair song from *The Story of Robert* (1987), given the full Talking Heads treatment by McGlashan's arrangement. McGlashan says: 'The song pretty much takes place in Robert's head as he stares at someone at [a] party. There's quite a bit of latent violence floating around in the story, much of it sensed by Robert, in terms of what he thinks might happen to him if he talks to the wrong woman, or says the wrong thing.' He continues:

> I'd been to Oamaru, and I was helping doing a writing project down there … and I went to a party and it got a bit weird, and I walked home and got stopped by a couple of people who said, 'You're not from around here, are you?' So from having quite a positive upbeat vision of life in small-town NZ it turned 180 degrees [into] … a piece … about memory … There's an event … that's unpicked by various people who were at this party, and there's a police interrogation of Robert, and we both alternate playing Robert, and playing the policemen … It was … partly about someone from a big town coming to a small town … but it's more about how you can be wrong about an event.

Sinclair: What songs were in *The Story of Robert*?

McGlashan: 'Claude Rains', 'Andy', the 'How You Doing' dance. The show started with the two of us rushing on to the stage, totally unaware of each other and we start talking to the audience, then we turn and recognize each other and we go into the dance.

Sinclair: Our major influence was not the kind of theatre I had done at Theatre Corporate but television and film ... Audiences are ... prepared to accept fast cutting ... like in a news program or a rock video. In *The Story of Robert,* we are demanding they follow something almost unintelligible because there are two people talking at once, as if someone was changing channels the whole time.[9]

McGlashan explains how this idea had already been tested in *Walkshort*:

Characters go through an action and explain what they are doing at the same time ... the camera plays the role of confessor for all those [film characters] who otherwise have no link. This led to *The Story of Robert,* in which one character is in real time and the other is commenting on him in documentary form. This creates tension between what the audience sees and what the audience is being told to see.[10]

Such filmic narrative techniques were to become a feature of McGlashan's writing in the Mutton Birds, in which ironic gaps open up between character and audience perspectives in songs like 'A Thing Well Made', 'White Valiant' (1990) and, in his solo work, 'Toy Factory Fire' (Don McGlashan 2006). Sinclair says:

When we began, we did not work with characters, just with aspects of ourselves, throwing away the idea of the theatre entirely. I think that's where a lot of the humour came from. We just appeared on the stage, as if we were two people from the audience ... Acting is now starting to come into our work – in *The Story of Robert* we actually play roles ... the difficult thing is to avoid institutionalizing our style. We always want to be surprised by what we do – to maintain a naivete.[11]

'Everyone Disappears' is from *The One That Got Away*: Neil, played by Sinclair, meets Glenda (Ward-Lealand) on a plane flight. They hit it off: this is the cue for a catchy, poppy song with a big, harmonized chorus. 'Neil is in a bad way, visiting a psychiatrist (Dr. Evans) played by … McGlashan. However, in the end "True Love" rather than … pills … cures Neil's anxiety.'[12] One reviewer describes the show's story as 'Pure Mills and Boon with an Auckland North Shore ambience – the world of the mock-Tudor or pseudo-Spanish suburban castles of the middle and lower middle classes with their concrete drives, their picture windows, perhaps a spa pool and … a front lawn.'[13] However, other commentators have emphasized The Front Lawn's ironic distance from suburbia:

> [T]heir work presents a sense of uncertainty about local culture … stumbling about in search of moorings … shifting … between a celebration of contemporary 'kiwi' culture and its critique. Any sense of local identity is no longer to be found … in the landscape, but hanging out amongst … the subdivisions and shopping malls. A whole new sensibility is needed to negotiate this environment: droll, ironic, streetwise.[14]

This contemporary sensibility was to be developed more fully in the 'slacker' characters of Sinclair's TV series and film *Topless Women Talk About Their Lives* (1995 and 1997).

'Coming Ready or Not' is also from *The One That Got Away*, and is also sung by Sinclair, with a similar intimate feel and subdued musical setting to 'Walk Around the House' and 'Tell Me What to Do.' 'They're going fishing, and they're falling in love and that's kind of meshed in with them catching a fish, they kind of get tangled up together' (from the CD liner notes).

This also helps explain the title of the show. The song features the sound of panting, suggesting pursuit.

'A Good Address' is from *The Washing Machine* (1987), which was partly a 'satire on consumerism [but also] also about fathers and sons and inheritance', says McGlashan. The song was described by one reviewer as 'like Kurt Weill visits Blockhouse Bay'.[15] Sinclair brought in the original idea, '[He] said, "What about a show where we're not banging on things; the actual objects … make a rhythm?"' and that led to having a washing machine actually working on stage which was a fucking hassle 'cos we had to get water on and off stage.' To write it, 'we made a tape of the cycle and played it as we wrote so we were working with the exact timing of it'.[16] In the show, McGlashan plays Roy, the father, and Sinclair, his son, Graeme, a gameshow host obsessed with consumer gadgetry.

> Sinclair: I fell in love with the washing machine and you married me to it.
>
> McGlashan: It got quite Fellini-esque.
>
> Sinclair: It was pretty dark.

The duo also developed a script for a fifty-minute TV film, entitled *The Wash Cycle*,[17] but it was never made. Possibly it was too critical of the corporates who were being asked to fund it. In 'A Good Address', Roy reminisces about the 1950s, often viewed as a time of post-war prosperity. The recording features a prominent theatre organ sound, immediately suggesting nostalgia. McGlashan says: 'The quarter-acre pavlova paradise wasn't something we were satirising … The anger in [*The Washing Machine*] was about the Chase Corporation knocking down old buildings and replacing them with car parks.'[18] Sinclair adds,

It was two versions of New Zealand, my character completely obsessed about buying things and the older father figure … representing … the gentler earlier times, when things didn't have to be new … you could hold on to them, like a good address was a thing, a place, that had some meaning … You could buy a house in those days … it's a dream that's gone.

'The Beautiful Things' is also from *The Washing Machine*, and is Graeme's demented anthem to consumerism: 'We buy and we are born again.' McGlashan says, 'The Beautiful Things' kind of sums up [*The Washing Machine*] 'cos it was right in the middle of the Rogernomics era, and the country was being stripped bare, kind of a "greed is good" ethos everywhere.' The accompanying video makes the satirical intent clear, while the keyboard riff ironically suggests contemporary urban lifestyle. The song also gains impetus from the duo firing off each other, with McGlashan singing while Sinclair features in a series of increasingly manic voiceovers.

'Queen Street' is from *The One That Got Away*: 'Neil tells of a chance meeting with Glenda, while … Dr. Evans worries that Neil is getting out of his depth' (from the CD liner notes). A catchy chorus with narrative verses about an encounter on Auckland's 'main drag', this song and 'A Good Address' continue the group's fascination with Auckland placenames, which culminated in the Mutton Birds' 'Dominion Road' (1992).

'Breakfast Anthem/Mess' is from *The Reason For Breakfast* (1986). In its original context, it accompanies the destruction of a breakfast table by rhythmic assault. 'We found it interesting', says Sinclair, 'to look at things people see every day, but from a different angle. We enjoy showing breakfast to people.'[19] A cover by the Australian Spooky Men's Chorale reveals hidden depths in the song. The massed male voices of the Chorale add a sense of grandeur lacking in the original.[20]

'Because She's Gone' is from *Linda's Body*, although the lyric in the film is 'Now she's gone'. The melody functions as a leitmotif in the film, and lacking that context robs this remake of its poignancy, though the synthesizer solo at the end is effectively creepy.

In 'Wedding Song' from *The Washing Machine,* 'Roy, finally reconciled to his son Graeme's insanity, marries him to the washing machine he adores' (from the CD liner notes). Melodically and harmonically, this is a reprise of 'A Good Address', effective as a finale to the show, and with some funny lines e.g. 'Do you take this man/To cherish you and install you, to put his dirty things inside you?' but arguably not so effective as a standalone track. Nevertheless, even if it lacks the effervescence of Six Volts, overall, the album is high quality, especially the writing.

Conclusion

It seems surprising that neither Front Lawn album has ever been remastered or reissued (perhaps a downside of self-release?). They fell between the cracks of the music industry, being neither slick enough for commercial radio, nor weird enough for alternative circles. Was student radio supportive of the group? 'Not terribly', says McGlashan, and Sinclair adds, 'We weren't cool in the music world because we were funny.' McGlashan adds, 'It was considered uncool to jump sideways out of music and do this other thing. The music scene … was pretty narrow … if you weren't doing one kind of thing, you were considered to be a dilettante … Record companies never saw dollar signs when they saw The Front Lawn.' However, McGlashan adds, 'I think that's changed … the scene's not … so rigid now, you've got groups like Flight of the Conchords, but nobody would say [now], "Oh that's uncool, why don't they just do x?"' Certainly the group did not want to be categorized as alternative, McGlashan opining, 'The world's full of people – especially artists – who feel they don't belong anywhere, and want to fill the airways, book and record stores with that sentiment. We could easily be part of that … but it's better not to be.'[21]

All the Front Lawn members have gone on to achieve in their chosen fields. Ward-Lealand is one of New Zealand's best-known stage actors, appearing in films (notably *Desperate Remedies* in 1993), and in 2020 she was named Kiwibank New Zealander of the Year. She 'has been a keen student and champion of Te Reo Māori since 2008, and in 2017 was gifted the name Te Atamira (The Stage) by Sir Tīmoti Kāretu and the late Prof Te Wharehuia Milroy.'[22] Sinclair is perhaps best known for *Topless Women Talk About Their Lives*, a comedy which started life as a series of four-minute episodes on TV3 in 1995, all featuring the same group of inner-city Auckland slackers. It then became a well-regarded film in 1997, characterized by its exuberant, zany, indeed Front Lawn-esque tone.[23] Both TV and film versions featured soundtracks by Flying Nun acts.[24] He directed two further features, *The Price of Milk* (1999) and *Toy Love* (2003) and appeared as Isildur in *The Lord of the Rings* before moving to Los Angeles. Most recently he has collaborated again with McGlashan on the TVNZ children's series *Kiri and Lou*.

In 1991, McGlashan formed the Mutton Birds, with David Long (guitar), Alan Gregg (bass) and Ross Burge (drums). They enjoyed commercial success in New Zealand with 'Nature', a cover of a 1970 track by The Fourmyula, reaching number four in New Zealand in late 1992. Subsequently the song was named in a 2001 APRA [Australasian Performing Rights Association] songwriters' poll as New Zealand's top song of all time, an achievement in which the Mutton Birds' version played an important but uncredited role.[25] Their self-titled, self-produced debut (Bag Records/EMI, 1992) continued themes first broached by The Front Lawn, albeit in a more conventional, guitar band-based context: 'White Valiant' extends the Kiwi Gothic of 'A Man and a Woman'; 'Dominion Road' continues the fascination with local culture. McGlashan says:

> I live really close to Dominion Road, and I was on a bus and I saw this guy who looked a bit confused … and as [we] passed him I made up a story … about how he could've got there: he was about my age, and if my life had gone a slightly different way, I could've ended up exactly like him.[26]

In a more sinister mode, 'A Thing Well Made' investigates NZ masculinity, consumerism and mass murder.[27] The album was commercially successful in New Zealand, reaching number two and remaining in the album charts for a year.[28] The group signed with Virgin Records and released a second album, *Salty*, in 1994, produced by Tchad Blake (Elvis Costello, Crowded House, Suzanne Vega). Standout tracks included the single 'Anchor Me', which won McGlashan an APRA Silver Scroll Award for songwriting, while 'Ngaire' extended McGlashan's gift for observation, featuring a narrator in an airport vainly awaiting the return of the titular heroine. Also, there were three quality contributions from bass player Alan Gregg, 'Wellington', 'Esther' and 'There's a Limit'.

The group relocated in London in 1994, and recorded probably their most consistent album, *Envy of Angels* (Virgin 1996) at Rockfield Studio in Wales with Hugh Jones (Echo and the Bunnymen, Teardrop Explodes, The Sound). The title track is a haunting exploration of landscape and colonization, refracted through a father–son relationship, while 'Along the Boundary' is a wonderful song about childhood in New Zealand. But Virgin Records dropped the group and their final studio album, *Rain, Steam and Speed* (Sssssh! Records 1999) was released independently as McGlashan returned to New Zealand, and the group broke up in 2000, although they reunited for some live shows in 2012.[29] McGlashan has continued as a solo act, releasing albums regularly: *Warm Hand* (Arch Hill Records, 2006), *Marvellous Year* (Arch Hill Records, 2009), *Lucky Stars* (self-released, 2015) and *Bright November Morning* (self-released, 2022). All of McGlashan's catalogue is available through his website.[30] In 2009 he was part of Seven Worlds Collide, a collaboration with musicians including Neil Finn, Johnny Marr and members of Wilco and Radiohead. He is also a prolific film composer, working with top directors like Jane Campion (*An Angel at my Table*, 1990) and Toa Fraser (*No. 2* [2006]; *Dean Spanley* [2008]). A McGlashan song from *No. 2*, 'Bathe in the River' became a local smash hit in 2006, in a version by Hollie Smith.[31] Undoubtedly, McGlashan is one of the major voices of New Zealand music.

What has been the influence of The Front Lawn? 'A huge number of people have said to me that "The Front Lawn was the best thing you were ever a part of"', says McGlashan. Ward-Lealand says: '[McGlashan and Sinclair were] a charmed duo, they had a similar sensibility … they really wanted to speak about us as New Zealanders … there was a real cultural cringe then … as if we were less than worthy … the work spoke to people's sense of self, our aotearoatanga … it was celebrating that.' The Front Lawn have certainly influenced some subsequent acts, such as Flight of the Conchords: 'Brett (Mackenzie) was a 13-year-old when he was ushering for our show, in the University Memorial Theatre, Wellington … it was tremendously inspiring for him', says Ward-Lealand. 'Jemaine Clement's father used to make our video copies, and that's how Jemaine got to see The Front Lawn … Apparently, he would make an extra copy for himself', says Sinclair. More broadly, the Lawn was part of a continuum of local, self-contained, multi-talented duos/trios, like the Conchords and the Topp Twins (with whom the Lawn appeared on several occasions). 'When we were on tour we literally took Don's guitar, my ukulele, Harry's squeeze box, two torches and our suits … We could've done the show anywhere … we were very self-contained', says Ward-Lealand. There is a local tradition of DIY adaptability which the Lawn fits into. They had an optimism that was lacking in local culture at the time. Partly this comes down to 'a humour that came out of the situation, it was never for a cheap laugh', says Ward-Lealand. Their comic style, once described as 'a dozen shades of deadpan'[32] fits well into the tradition of Fred Dagg/John Clarke and Taika Waititi, albeit leavened with music.

Musically, The Front Lawn fitted between classic NZ songwriters like Tim and Neil Finn, Dave Dobbyn and more recently Bic Runga on the one hand, musicians who are certainly known to drop the odd local inflection into their work; and the indie music of the 1980s and 1990s, especially Flying Nun – indeed McGlashan has worked with a number of Flying Nun artists, including myself and Shayne Carter, who plays in his current band, The Others.[33] Although indie embraced the whole gamut of alternative styles, a common theme was a preoccupation with boundaries and generic correctness: indie's 'counterhegemonic aims could only be maintained ... by erecting exclusionary barriers around the culture'.[34] For example, some indie guitar bands' material was identified as 'pure pop' – implying distance from commercial pop, but also from 'rockism' – the traditional association of rock music with machismo.[35] This stylistic restriction can also be read in political terms, as against commercialization on the one hand, and sexism and racism on the other, both of which became coded as stylistic excess: a guitar solo was 'macho', a reggae rhythm too 'black'. In NZ indie, stylistic restriction was particularly marked. McGlashan remarked of the Mutton Birds: 'It's necessary to limit myself ... Working in a band is a process of subtracting the bits that no longer fit everybody's ideas of how the music ought to sound. The set of things that everyone feels comfortable with is necessarily refined'.[36] This is a different aesthetic to The Front Lawn, although it is prefigured in some of McGlashan's comments about songwriting. While I admire the Mutton Birds, there was something special about The Front Lawn – their openness to different approaches, and their fusion of different media.

McGlashan remains an eloquent spokesman for local culture:

> When you grow up in New Zealand, you hear a lot of people singing at you through TV and radio, in an American accent or an English accent ... about places you've never seen, and that leads to a feeling that maybe it's strange to write about your own place. Nothing could be more normal. Writing about your own place is the easiest thing to do ... it's what you know the best.[37]

Lawn clippings

There was nothing subeditors in the 1980s liked better than fashioning excruciating puns and wordplays out of The Front Lawn's name. Here is a selection, which I gleaned from a box of 'lawn' [press] clippings lent to me by the group:

Front Lawn grows (after they added a member) (Patrick Smith, *Auckland Star*, 6 April 1989, 8).

Green green grass of home (Jennifer Little, *Dominion Sunday Times*, 30 April 1989, 15).

Evergreen Lawn in top form (Susan Budd, *Dominion*, 15 May 1989, 6).

This lot will mow you over (*Tearaway,* June 1989).

May they grow long (*Auckland Star*, 1 June 1989, 13).

Front Lawn in clover (*Auckland Star*, 5 May 1988).

Lawnmower chorus (*New Zealand Times*, 7 July 1985, 28).

To mow them is to love them (Peter Allison, *Metro*, July 1990, 92–101).

Secondary growth (Antonius Papaspiropoulos, *Evening Post*, 26 April 1990, 31–2).

Lawn to run (Peter Allison, *Metro*, May 1989, 39).

Front Lawn back (not captioned).

(continued)

The Front Lawn timeline – a potted history

April–June 1985 – devised *Songs and Stories from The Front Lawn*.

July–August – first national tour (sponsored by the Students Arts Council). The *NZ Listener* enthused: 'This show, with its strong positive statement of gentle male energy, left me feeling invigorated and refreshed. It felt like seeing the birth of a new vaudeville. I saw The Front Lawn in a coffee lounge, but [they] should probably live in a caravan and perform in shopping malls everywhere. They're that good.'[38] Sinclair responded: 'I don't know about this "new vaudeville" business … there's a long history of this sort of thing in New Zealand, going back to the days of Blerta, Red Mole and now the Topp Twins – people who have combined music and theatre and comedy.'[39]

December – late night season, Theatre Corporate, Auckland.

January 1986 – wrote *The Reason for Breakfast*.

March – debuted at Little Maidment Theatre, Auckland; Depot Theatre, Wellington International Festival of the Arts. The *Dominion* raved, 'the hit of this busy three weeks has been the work of Harry Sinclair and Don McGlashan … you will hear much more of this Auckland-based piece of Kiwi mesmerism'.[40]

October–November – national tour (this is when I first saw them).

December – made video for 'I'm Right', directed by Grant Campbell.

January–March 1987 – wrote and made *Walkshort*, directed by William Toepfer (Toepfer went on to devise the premise of *Popstars*, which became an international reality TV franchise).

April – wrote *The Story of Robert*.

May – the duo debuted in Australia at Belvoir Street, Sydney. Sinclair said: 'No agent in New Zealand has ever phoned us up. In Australia we were phoned up by 15 different agents. It was great to be able to say, "We have been managing ourselves for quite a while and we like it that way."'[41]

June – wrote *The Washing Machine*.

September – Spoleto Festival, Melbourne, where *The Story of Robert* and *The Reason for Breakfast* were performed.

October–November – third national tour.

December – Southern Regional Arts Council tour.

January–May 1988 – wrote and made *The Lounge Bar*.

March – Melbourne Comedy Festival.

April – wrote 'Monster World Tour' show.

May/June – fourth national tour (featuring *The Reason for Breakfast*).

July – began work on the album, *Songs From The Front Lawn*.

August – Their debut at the Edinburgh Festival: 'After … *Crocodile Dundee* it is refreshing that some sophisticated, intelligent humour has come out of the Antipodes at last. The Front Lawn … are in fact from New Zealand, presumably how they escaped contamination.'[42] *The Independent* wrote: 'It's as if Talking

(continued)

Heads had met Men at Work in a bar with Ionesco and decided to party.'[43]

September – played Aarhus Festival, Denmark, Pick of the Fringe Season at Donmar Warehouse, London.

October – The group's US debut at Dance Theatre Workshop, New York. 'Party talk, snapshots, breakfast – commonplace events – take on new resonances … in the performance art of The Front Lawn.'[44]

November – the group wins *The Independent*'s 'Best of Edinburgh Festival' and do a season at the Half Moon Theatre in Stepney Green, London.

February–March 1989 – recorded *Songs From The Front Lawn*.

April – wrote *The One That Got Away*.

May–July – *The One That Got Away* national tour (Palmerston North, Wellington, Auckland, Christchurch, Dunedin). 'Unlike previous shows, which were a collection of brilliant and funny sketches interspersed with songs, this is a coherent play … another great show', said Susan Budd at the *Dominion*.[45] 'The most important thing about their latest comedy is that they are prepared to experiment', said Laurie Atkinson of the *Evening Post*,[46] while Patrick Smith praised 'a freshness and unselfconscious vitality that is seldom seen on the New Zealand stage'.[47] For Dominic Roskrow at the *NZ Herald*, the show was 'living proof … that genius is simplicity itself'.[48]

June – *Songs From The Front Lawn* released.

August – UK tour, Edinburgh Festival, Perth, London (Pick of the Fringe). In *The Scotsman* McGlashan compared the show to 'a bunch of people trying to do *West Side Story* with no budget'. However, the article continues, 'Don't be put off by Kiwi offhandedness. This a second year of quality performance from [The Front Lawn]'.[49] Even the UK music press was picking up on the group: 'Unless you want your life to be a total waste go and be dazzled', said the *NME*.[50] The group included a map of the upper North Island in the programme for the benefit of Northern Hemisphere audiences unfamiliar with local placenames in *The One That Got Away*.

September–October – US tour (Philadelphia, Minneapolis, and New York). In Philadelphia, the show was described as 'a delightful entertainment' and 'a comic mix of story and song'.[51]

March–April 1990 – Melbourne Comedy Festival. *Melbourne In Press noted*: 'The acting is fabulous … [The Front Lawn] are an extremely polished and talented trio, and those who were worried about the recent addition of a woman to the group can relax; Jennifer Ward-Lealand is just terrific.'[52]

April–May – Memorial Theatre, Wellington.

Notes

Chapter 1

1 John Lahr (ed.), *The Orton Diaries* (London: Methuen, 1968), 74.

2 Murray Edmond, *Then It Was Now Again: Selected Critical Writing* (Pokeno, New Zealand: Atanui Press, 2014), 97; Annabelle Melzer, *Latest Rage: The Big Drum: Dada and Surrealist Performance* (Ann Arbor: Ann Arbor Research Press, 1980), 60.

3 Edmond, 98.

4 James Belich, *Paradise Reforged: A History of the New Zealanders from the 1880s to the Year 2000* (Auckland: Penguin Press, 2001).

5 Nick Perry, *Dominion of Signs: Television, Advertising and Other New Zealand Fictions* (Auckland: Auckland University Press, 1994), 46.

6 Ibid., 100; Michelle Keown, '"He Iwi Kotahi Tatou?": Nationalism and Cultural Identity in Maori Film', in *Contemporary New Zealand Cinema: From New Wave to Blockbusters*, ed. Ian Conrich and Stuart Murray (London: I. B. Taurus, 2008), 197–210.

7 Jean-Pierre Mignon and Katharine Sturak, 'The Front Lawn: An Interview with Don McGlashan and Harry Sinclair', *Ant News*, February 1988, 5.

8 Robert Muldoon, 'Why We Stand with Our Mother Country', *The Times*, 20 May 1982, 14.

9 Michael King, *Being Pakeha: An Encounter with New Zealand and the Maori Renaissance* (Auckland: Hodder & Stoughton, 1985), 161.

10 J.G.A. Pocock, *The Discovery of Islands: Essays in British History* (Cambridge: Cambridge University Press, 2005), 13; Stuart Murray, *Never a Soul at Home: New Zealand Literary Nationalism and the 30s* (Wellington: Victoria University Press, 1998).

11 Keith Sinclair, *A Destiny Apart: New Zealand's Search for National Identity* (Wellington: Allen & Unwin, 1985).

12 Jock Phillips, *A Man's Country? The Image of the Pakeha Male – A History* (Auckland: Penguin, 1987); Kai Jensen, *Whole Men: The Masculine Tradition in New Zealand Literature* (Auckland: Auckland University Press, 1996). The 'man alone' trope was named for John Mulgan's novel *Man Alone* (Hamilton: Paul's Book Arcade, 1960). The man alone has a complex relationship with cultural identity, being on the one hand related to an ideal of pioneering manhood in the bush, and hence to the Kiwi bloke; but also to an international tradition of modernist alienation – the outsider, see Baxter's *The Fire and the Anvil: Notes on Modern Poetry* (Wellington: New Zealand University Press, 1955), 70–2.

13 Harry Sinclair, 'Self-Portrait: Harry Sinclair', 24 November 2021, https://www.newsroom.co.nz/self-portrait-harry-sinclair.

14 'Making Music – Don McGlashan', 2005, https://www.nzonscreen.com/title/making-music-don-mcglashan-2005?collection=the-don-mcglashan-collection.

15 The quotes from McGlashan and Sinclair all derive from Zoom interviews recorded on 20 August and 16 September 2021, unless otherwise stated. In a 1988 interview with Phil Twyford, Sinclair stated that he was playing the school's headmaster, not his father, but the general fratricidal intention seems consistent: 'Front Lawn Clover', *Auckland Star*, 5 May 1988, B1. Sinclair has discussed how his father's affairs led to his parents' divorce, in 'Self-Portrait'.

16 Wade Churton, *'Have You Checked the Children?' Punk and Post-punk Music in New Zealand, 1977–1981* (Christchurch: Put Your Foot Down Publishing, 2000), 35; Roger Shepherd, *In Love With These Times: My Life with Flying Nun Records* (Auckland: HarperCollins, 2016), 33, 36.

17 Michel de Certeau, *The Practice of Everyday Life* (San Diego: University of California Press, 1984), ix.

18 Paul Hagan, 'Morning Ritual', *NZ Listener*, 29 November 1986, 54.

19 John Dix, *Stranded in Paradise* (Wellington: Paradise Publications, 1988), 206.

20 Gary Steel, 'Don McGlashan – Profile', 21 August 2019, https://www.audioculture.co.nz/people/don-mcglashan.

21 Gareth Shute, 'Reggae Aotearoa Timeline', 28 January 2019, https://www.audioculture.co.nz/articles/reggae-aotearoa-timeline.

22 Margi Mellsop, quoted in Matt Elliott, *Kiwi Jokers: The Rise and Rise of NZ Comedy* (Auckland: HarperCollins, 1997), 89.

23 Mignon and Sturak.

24 Martin Flanagan, 'Performer Makes the Everyday an Artform', *The Age*, 19 April 1990, 11.

25 Andrew Clifford, 'Five Rhythm Works', CD liner notes, EM Records, 2016.

26 'Rhythmanalysis', in *A Dictionary of Human Geography*, ed. Alisdair Rogers, Noel Castree and Rob Kitchin (Oxford: Oxford University Press, 2013).

27 Steel.

28 Mignon and Sturak.

29 Russell Baillie, 'The Don of Rock', *New Zealand Herald*, 22–23 May 1999: D5.

30 'Don't Fight It Marsha, It's Bigger Than Both of Us' video (Andrew Shaw, 1981), https://www.nzonscreen.com/title/dont-fight-it-marsha-its-bigger-than-both-of-us-1981.

31 Dix, 280.

32 Hagan.

33 Mignon and Sturak.

34 Ibid.

Chapter 2

1 Virginia S. Jenkins, 'A Green Velvety Carpet: The Front Lawn in America', *Journal of American Culture* 17, no. 3 (1994): 43.

2 Ibid.

3 Sarah Marusek, 'Lawnscape: Semiotics of Space, Spectacle, and Ownership', *Social Semiotics* 22, no. 4 (2012): 447.

4 'Lawnmower Chorus Cultural Expression', *New Zealand Times*, 7 July 1985, 28 (no author listed).

5 It should be noted however, that the group did use amplification on occasion. Some leads can be seen in Figure 1.2, and other pictures from that roll show microphones being used.

6 Mignon and Sturak.

7 Phil Twyford, 'Front Lawn in Clover', *Auckland Star*, 5 May 1988, B1.

8 Mandi and Debbi Gibbs, 'Songs and Stories from The Front Lawn', *Book of BiFim*, August 1985 (no page numbers).

9 The Front Lawn, 'I'm Right', https://www.youtube.com/watch?v=BKdGGL6IinE.

10 *Walkshort*, 1987, https://www.nzonscreen.com/title/walkshort-1987.

11 Michel de Certeau, 'Walking in the City', in *The Cultural Studies Reader*, ed. Simon During (London: Routledge, 1993), 158.

12 Henri Bergson, *Laughter: An Essay on the Meaning of the Comic* (Mineola, NY: Dover Publications, 2005), 24.

13 'A Dozen Different Shades of Deadpan', *The Press*, 15 May 1987, 15.

14 *The Lounge Bar*, 1988, https://www.nzonscreen.com/title/the-lounge-bar-1988.

15 'The Front Lawn – Don Visits Harry', n.d., https://www.youtube.com/watch?v=r3Zvd4YoK9Q.

16 Don McGlashan, email communication, 8 September 2021.

17 Of these groups, probably Split Enz had the most in common with The Front Lawn, favouring a theatrical self-presentation, and being 'an eccentric act that came out of NZ. That was encouraging' (Harry Sinclair, quoted in Martin Flanagan, 'Performer Makes the Everyday an Artform', *The Age*, 19 April 1990, 11).

18 Dix, 280.

19 Paul Hagan, 'Three's Company', *NZ Listener*, 10 June 1989, 34.

20 Richard Brent Turner, *Jazz Religion, the Second Line, and Black New Orleans* (Bloomington: Indiana University Press, 2009); all Long quotes are from a Zoom interview recorded on 6 September 2021.

21 'Front Lawn, Six Volts Shock Big Town Values', *Capital Times*, 21 February 1989, 3.

22 Churton, 32.

23 Mascot was home of Warrior Records and reggae band Herbs. Flying Nun bands also recorded there, including Sneaky Feelings, The Chills, The Verlaines and Snapper.

24 However, in 1989, Lealand told a different story: 'They rang from London in October (1988) to ask if I'd like to join them', Patrick Smith. 'Front Lawn Grows', *Auckland Star*, 6 April 1989, 8 (of Breakout).

25 All quotes from Ward-Lealand are from a Zoom interview, recorded on 21 August 2021, unless otherwise noted.

26 Long now plays in a band called Teeth (no relation of the late 1980s Auckland band who released an EP on Flying Nun), with Tom Callwood and Luke Buda from the Phoenix Foundation.

27 Matthew Bannister, *White Boys, White Noise: Masculinities and Indie Guitar Rock* (UK: Ashgate, 2006).

Chapter 3

1 A very rough copy can be found on YouTube, https://www.youtube.com/watch?v=bdmmWjkpshM.

2 In his album review, Colin Hogg refers to a 'Kiwi strum' though he relates it to 'How You Doing'. 'May They Grow Long', *Auckland Star*, 1 June 1989, 13.

3 Paul Gilroy, *The Black Atlantic: Modernity and Double Consciousness* (Cambridge, MA: Harvard University Press, 1993). 'The Black Atlantic' is the idea that black popular culture cannot be located in a particular time or place, due to the historic black diaspora, which began with slavery.

Rather it circulates between Europe, Africa and the New World. More recently, Robbie Shilliam has applied a similar idea to the Southern Hemisphere in *The Black Pacific: Anti-colonial Struggles and Oceanic Connection* (London: Bloomsbury, 2015).

4   Michael Brown, 'Making Our Own – Two Ethnographies of the Vernacular in New Zealand Music: Tramping Club Singsongs and the Māori Guitar Strumming Style' (PhD diss., Victoria University of Wellington, NZ, 2012), https://notunlikeatrumpet.files.wordpress.com/2019/09/brown-phd-2012.pdf.

5   Simon Sweetman, 'Split Enz', 2009, http://www.stuff.co.nz/entertainment/blogs/blog-on-the-tracks/2353006/Split-Enz.

6   Nick Bollinger, *100 Essential New Zealand Albums* (Wellington: Awa Press, 2009), 79.

7   Chris Bourke, *Crowded House: Something So Strong* (South Melbourne: Macmillan, 1997), 76; Simon Sweetman, '10 of My Favourite New Zealand Songs', 2011, http://www.stuff.co.nz/entertainment/blogs/blog-on-the-tracks/5050899/10-of-myfavourite-New-Zealand-songs.

8   Nick Bollinger, 'Bro Strum', *New Zealand Listener*, 30 November 1996, 42; John Ferguson, 'Acts Aim for Global Impact – Strength of Local Music Scene Sets Stage for International Breakthrough', *Billboard*, 30 November 2002, 45.

9   Sally Bodkin-Allen, 'Welcome Home: Music, Rugby, and Place', in *Home, Land and Sea: Situating Music in Aotearoa New Zealand*, ed. Glenda Keam and Tony Mitchell (North Shore: Pearson, 2011), 70.

10   Brown, 200.

11   Paul Magan, 'Morning Ritual', *NZ Listener*, 29 November 1986, 54.

12 Chad Taylor, 'Stakes in the Grass – Words from The Front Lawn', *Rip It Up*, May 1989, 8.

13 Nick Bollinger, 'Substance Beneath', *NZ Listener*, 17 June 1989, 54.

14 Tony Green, 'The Front Lawn – Songs from The Front Lawn', *The Press*, 16 June 1989, 28; Colin Hogg, 'May They Grow Long'. It should be noted that Hogg's review is very favourable, as are those by Redmer Yska (*Dominion*, 4 June 1989, and Paul Casserly [*Monitor,* June 1989]).

15 Bollinger, 140.

16 'There Is No Depression in New Zealand' video, (Andrew Shaw, 1981) https://www.nzonscreen.com/title/there-is-no-depression-in-new-zealand-1981; John Wilson, 'Nation and Government – Nationhood and Identity', in *Te Ara – The Encyclopedia of New Zealand*, accessed 26 July 2018, www.TeAra.govt.nz/en/nation-and-government/page–9.

17 Nick Perry, *Hyperreality and Global Culture* (New York: Routledge, 1998).

18 *Linda's Body*, 1990, https://www.nzonscreen.com/title/lindas-body-1990.

19 Rangi is played by Ramai Hayward (pioneer NZ filmmaker, spouse of Udall Hayward). Another well-known Māori actor, Wi Kuki Kaa, plays the ghost of her husband, Hemi.

20 'Haere Mai', by Bill Wolfgramm, featuring vocal by Daphne Walker (Tanza 1955), https://music.youtube.com/watch?v=6aFru1QwCyU&list=RDAMVM6aFru1QwCyU; written by Sam Freedman – https://www.youtube.com/watch?v=03U2ocJsiGs.

21 Tia DeNora, 'Music as a Technology of the Self', *Poetics* 27, no. 1 (1999): 31–56.

22 Philip Tagg, *Everyday Tonality: Towards a Tonal Theory of What Most People Hear* (New York and Montreal: Mass Media Scholar's Press, 2009).

23 Slavoj Žižek, 'Melancholy and the Act', *Critical Inquiry* 26, no. 4 (Summer, 2000): 662.

24 Ibid., 659.

25 It is on *Salty* (The Mutton Birds, Virgin 1994).

26 Blair French, 'Locating Linda's Body', *Illusions* 16 (1991): 11–14. French argues that *Linda's Body* is quite conventional in terms of its gendered gaze on the female body.

27 Frank Sargeson, *Collected Stories* (London: MacGibbon & Kee, 1965), 170.

28 Ibid., 208.

29 Kate Burridge and Margaret Florey, '"Yeah-No He's a Good Kid": A Discourse Analysis of Yeah-No in Australian English', *Australian Journal of Linguistics* 22, no. 2 (2002): 149.

30 Joel MacManus, 'Why Do New Zealanders Say "eh" So Much?' 29 June 2019, https://www.stuff.co.nz/national/113796639/why-do-new-zealanders-say-eh-so-much.

31 The Royal Antediluvian Order of Buffaloes 'originated in Great Britain in 1822. The Grand Lodge of New Zealand was established in 1922', https://natlib.govt.nz/records/22389752.

32 Mignon and Sturak.

33 *Strangely Familiar: Design and Everyday Life*, ed. Andrew Blauvelt (Minneapolis, MN: Walker Art Center, 2003).

34 'The Double Standard in the Bike Bridge Backlash', 15 August 2021, https://www.rnz.co.nz/national/programmes/mediawatch/audio/2018808153/the-double-standard-in-the-bike-bridge-backlash.

35 Phillips.

36 Nick Braae, 'Don McGlashan and Local Authenticity', in *The Cambridge Companion to the Singer-Songwriter*, ed. Katherine Williams and Justin A. Williams (Cambridge: Cambridge University Press, 2016), 307.

37 Ibid., 312.

38 Maurice Gee, *Going West* (London: Faber & Faber, 1992), 69.

39 Gordon Spittle, *Counting the Beat: A History of New Zealand Song* (Wellington: GP Publications, 1997), 123.

40 David Gans, *Talking Heads* (New York: Avon, 1985), 52.

41 Simon Frith, *Music for Pleasure: Essays in the Sociology of Pop* (London: Basil Blackwell, 1988), 98–101; Gareth Palmer, 'Bruce Springsteen and Masculinity', in *Sexing the Groove: Popular Music and Gender*, ed. Sheila Whiteley (London: Routledge, 1997), 115.

42 Graham Reid, 'City's Lost Heart Saddens Stage Duo', *NZ Herald*, 5 May 1988, 15.

43 Lindsay Shelton, *The Selling of New Zealand Movies* (Wellington: Awa Press, 2005), 81.

44 Jane Campion, 'Different Complexions', in *Film in Aotearoa New Zealand*, ed. Jonathan Dennis and Jan Beiringa (Wellington: Victoria University Press, 1992), 95.

45 Quoted in Roger Horrocks, 'A Small Room with Large Windows: Film Making in NZ', in *New Zealand Film: An Illustrated History*, ed. Diane Pivac, Frank Stark, and Lawrence McDonald (Wellington: Te Papa Press, 2011), 5.

46 Chris Bourke, *Crowded House: Something so Strong* (Sydney: Macmillan, 1997), 112–13.

47 Bollinger, 142.

48 Robin Denselow, 'Paul Simon's Graceland: The Acclaim and the Outrage', *The Guardian*, 19 April 2012, https://www.theguardian.com/music/2012/apr/19/paul-simon-graceland-acclaim-outrage.

49 'Don't Go', Right Left and Centre, 1985, https://www.nzonscreen.com/title/dont-go-1985.

50 Tim Davey and Horst Puschmann, *Kiwi Rock* (New Zealand: Kiwi Rock Publications, 1996), 60.

51 Keith Sinclair, *A Destiny Apart: New Zealand's Search for National Identity* (Wellington: Allen & Unwin, 1985), 125.

52 Misha Kavka, Jennifer Lawn, and Mary Paul, *Gothic NZ: The Darker Side of Kiwi Culture* (Dunedin: Otago University Press, 2006).

53 Bill Pearson, *Fretful Sleepers and Other Essays* (Auckland: Heinemann, 1974); Gordon McLauchlan, *The Passionless People* (Auckland: Cassell, 1976). See also a contemporary report 'Passionless People' https://www.nzonscreen.com/title/passionless-people-1976.

54 Stella Gibbons, *Cold Comfort Farm* (London: Longman, 1932).

55 'Ska', in *Encyclopedia of Popular Music*, ed. Colin Larkin (Oxford Music Online: Oxford University Press, 2016).

56 'Return of the Front Lawn', 31 March 2019, https://www.rnz.co.nz/national/programmes/standing-room-only/audio/2018688909/return-of-the-front-lawn.

57 Cooke, Patricia, 'Journey of Skill and Wit', *Evening Post*, 16 May 1989, 15.

Chapter 4

1 The NZ charts site charts.org.nz records the album as charting at 40 on 18 June 1989. Total sales of the album by 4 January 1990 were 2344 (374 CDs, 787 LPs, 1183 tapes), according to a Front Lawn press release, (which erroneously

records the total as 3544, and exaggerates the chart positions of the album and single). Another Front Lawn document from June 1990 lists total sales as 823 CDs, 1290 LPs and 2174 tapes, totalling 4287. These are good sales figures for a locally produced, independent record in New Zealand at the time.

2 Sadly, none of these clips seem to be available. Nor are there videos of any shows. McGlashan: 'We were actively against video-ing the shows, so no videos exist of any shows except *The One That Got Away*' (and they don't think much of that, so it is unlikely to become available).

3 Sally Markham, 'Double Bill Makes an Impressive Festival Opening', *Dominion Sunday Times*, 4 August 1991, 25. The Topp Twins are twin sister duo Jools and Lynda Topp, lesbian folk singer/comedians who have been popular in New Zealand since the late 1970s. On their significance, see Matthew Bannister, '"Bush camp"? The Topp Twins and Antipodean Camp', *The Australasian Journal of Popular Culture* 4, no. 1 (2015): 3–14.

4 Gary Steel, 'Don McGlashan – Part One', https://www.audioculture.co.nz/articles/don-mcglashan-part-one.

5 Gareth Shute, *NZ Rock 1987–2007* (Auckland: Random House, 2008), 33–4.

6 'The Beautiful Things', 1993, https://www.nzonscreen.com/title/the-beautiful-things-1993.

7 Robert Ward, 'Front Lawn to Give up Their Live Show Turf', *NZ Herald*, 30 April 1993, section 2, 3.

8 Elliott, 89.

9 Mignon and Sturak, 5.

10 Ibid.

11 Ibid.

12 Edmond, 102.

13 Ibid.

14 French, 11.

15 Ward.

16 Mignon and Sturak.

17 I found a copy of it in the box of press clippings Don McGlashan supplied me with.

18 Austin Mitchell, *The Half-Gallon Quarter-Acre Pavlova Paradise* (Wellington: Whitcombe and Tombs, 1972). A number of books from this period reflected a critical concern with NZ identity, see also McLauchlan (1976) and Donna Awatere, *Maori Sovereignty* (Auckland: Broadsheet, 1984).

19 Hagan.

20 'Mess Song', 2018, https://www.youtube.com/watch?v=nST-axb7ARc.

21 Clare Pasley, 'Under Pressure', *RTR Countdown*, May 1989, 43.

22 https://www.jenniferwardlealand.com/.

23 Excerpts of both film and TV series can be viewed at https://www.nzonscreen.com/title/topless-women-talk-about-their-lives-1997.

24 Various, *Topless Women Talk about Their Lives* (Flying Nun Records, 1997), https://www.discogs.com/release/369495-Various-Topless-Women-Talk-About-Their-Lives.

25 Nick Braae, 'Musical Anti-Virtuosity in New Zealand's *Nature's Best*', *Popular Music and Society* 41, no. 2 (2018): 176–93.

26 'Making Music – Don McGlashan'.

27 Matthew Bannister, 'A Thing Well Made? NZ Settler Identity and Pakeha Masculinity in the Work of Don McGlashan', *Perfect Beat* 8, no. 1 (2006): 22–49.

28 https://charts.nz/search.asp?cat=a&search=mutton+birds.

29 *An Angel at My Table* (Jane Campion, 1990); *Cinema of Unease* (Sam Neill and Judy Rymer, 1995); *No. 2* (Toa Fraser, 2005); *Dean Spanley* (Toa Fraser, 2008); *The Dead Lands* (Toa Fraser, 2014). A comprehensive list of McGlashan's film and TV work is available at https://www.nzonscreen.com/collection/the-don-mcglashan-collection.

30 https://donmcglashan.com.

31 https://www.nzonscreen.com/title/bathe-in-the-river-2006.

32 *The Press*, 15 May 1987, 15.

33 I played lead guitar with the Mutton Birds in 1999, and they recorded one of my songs (originally recorded with Flying Nun act Sneaky Feelings) 'Not to Take Sides', which is on *Flock: The Best of the Mutton Birds* (EMI, 2002). I wrote extensively about McGlashan's music and its relation to NZ culture in Bannister, 22–49.

34 David Hesmondhalgh, 'Indie: The Institutional Politics and Aesthetics of a Popular Music Genre', *Cultural Studies* 13 (1999): 38.

35 Roy Shuker, *Key Concepts in Popular Music* (London: Routledge, 1998), 104; Simon Reynolds, *Blissed Out: The Raptures of Rock* (London: Serpent's Tail, 1990), 23. Alan Gregg's Mutton Birds' material fitted the pure pop template, whereas McGlashan's material was more 'rock'.

36 Matthew Bannister, 'Don McGlashan: Touching the Green, Green Grass of Home', *Music in New Zealand* 36 (Summer 1999–2000): 51.

37 'Making Music – Don McGlashan'.

38 Paul Hagan, 'Picnics on the Fringe', *NZ Listener*, 5 October 1985, 65–7.

39 Jonathan Dowling, 'Mowin' 'em down', *NZ Herald*, 12 November 1986 (incomplete, based on press clipping).

40 Ralph McAllister, *Dominion*, March 1986 (incomplete, based on press clipping).

41 Twyford, B1.

42 Rory Knight Bruce, *The Scotsman*, 20 August 1988 (incomplete, based on press clipping).

43 Alex Renton, 'Front Lawn', *The Independent*, 15 September 1988.

44 Jon Pareles, 'From New Zealand, a Breakfast Fantasy', *New York Times*, 15 October 1988, 1018.

45 'Evergreen Front Lawn in Top Form', *Dominion*, 15 May 1989, 6.

46 Laurie Atkinson, 'Bold Experiment Thrills Audience', *Evening Post*, 16 May 1989, 33.

47 'It's a gem – don't miss it', *Auckland Star*, 31 May 1989, A14.

48 Dominic Roskrow, 'Proof of Genius', *NZ Herald*, 31 May 1989, 21.

49 *The Scotsman*, 28 August 1989 (incomplete, based on press clipping).

50 Andy Fyfe, *NME*, 16 September 1989, 62.

51 Douglas Keating, 'A Comic Mix of Song and Story', *The Philadelphia Inquirer*, 7 October 1989 (incomplete, based on press clipping).

52 Fiona Scott-Norman, 'The Front Lawn – The One That Got Away', *In Press*, Melbourne, 4 April 1990, 37.

Index

General